OLD IS <u>NOT</u>
A FOUR-LETTER WORD!

Old is <u>Not</u>
a Four-Letter Word!

New Moods and Meanings in Aging

JEAN BEAVEN ABERNETHY

ABINGDON PRESS

Nashville   New York

OLD IS NOT A FOUR-LETTER WORD!

Copyright © 1975 by Abingdon Press

The lines from "purer than purest pure" by e e cummings in
Complete Poems 1912-1962 are reprinted with permission from
Harcourt Brace Jovanovich, and MacGibbon and Kee.

Library of Congress Cataloging in Publication Data

Abernethy, Jean Beaven, 1912-
  Old is not a four-letter word!
  1. Aging. 2. Aged—United States. 3. Aged—Conduct of life.
4. Self-realization. I. Title.
HQ1064.U5A62   301.43′5′0973   74-19391

ISBN 0-687-28749-9

MANUFACTURED BY THE PARTHENON PRESS AT
NASHVILLE, TENNESSEE, UNITED STATES OF AMERICA

*To my husband whose love
has encouraged me in the
freedom to be myself.*

CONTENTS

GROWING OLD TODAY MEANS GROWING NEW

OUR PRESENT OFFERS US FRESH OPPORTUNITIES

OUR PAST CAN TEACH US

OUR FUTURE STIRS UP NEW VISTAS

GROWING OLD TODAY
MEANS GROWING NEW

CHAPTER 1

Growing Old: Invitation to Personal Choice

Thanks be for aging.

Without aging, we would be like we were back there when we were born—limited, inexperienced, without focus or coordination, breadth or depth.

Whereas with aging—the piling up of day after day and of year after year—has come the rich and multiform variety to be found inside each one of us. It is because we have aged that we have moved from the simple to the complex, from the diffuse to the distinct, from the inarticulate to the articulate.

Thanks be for aging.

But most of us are not thankful at all. It never occurs to us that what we are doing everyday is aging. Until one day we do realize it because others look at us and say, "You are aging." Yet when that happens, strangely enough, we are embarrassed by it. We are more than embarrassed. We become defensive. Some, even, experience a minor kind of panic as though they had passed a point of no return. For to be called an aging person is to hear a patronizing and derogatory remark about oneself; to know that society (our society, at least) no longer sees us as integral and in the midst of life—useful, needed and belonging—but more and more off to one side with the mainstream going on somewhere else.

But why? Who is to say where the mainstream of life does or does not flow? How can aging, which we do all of our lives and which continues right up to the end to be the rich source of the variety that is in us—how can it suddenly, and at some point along the line, become of no value? What is this happening called "old," which punctuates the aging process by downgrading the image we have of ourselves?

This book is an attempt to examine that happening and challenge that downgrading, not by pretty remarks to bolster self-esteem but by trying to detail the authenticity and ongoing value of the aging we all experience during the last third of the life-span. It hopes to show that, for those of us who are no longer young, and no longer middle-aged, the ingredients for powerful human drama are still ours; that interesting, exciting, and significant things happen for us now as they did earlier. In far greater measure than most of us are ready for, these closing years of ours give us the freedom to choose and to grow, to seek and to find.

But freedom may overwhelm us. Loneliness may even keep us from going outside the front door and finding one another. And fear, if it has its way, may not let go its grip long enough for us to see ourselves as we might be.

What would be warming and encouraging would be to find a few others who might want to meet together with us around the sincerely meant, and the simply said statement, "This is where I am in the experience of late aging; where are you?" For in saying this, and in the listening and learning that would follow, answers to our own particular dilemmas—answers already present in us somewhere, but perhaps not fully heard, might well be called forth.

This book is written around that hope. Perhaps a few friends decide to meet—or a few acquaintances, who see each other often but have never explored together in any depth things that matter. They would like to talk about such things (in this case, about growing old with its mix of moods and meanings), but they are not sure where others are in their thinking. This book might serve as an agreed upon starting line, and the group could take it from there. Having read it, they would use the material presented here not only as the basis for their gatheredness, but as the mutual stimulus which could spark their several imaginations.

Or if small group sharing is not feasible, the material here can set in motion a kind of dialogue within the reader himself or herself. There is a wealth of emotions and ideas inside us, born of this new image we have of ourselves as "aging persons." We need to tap this wealth, bring it to the surface, and examine it. If, as we say, we are growing old, what precisely is it we are saying to ourselves when we say that? What do we mean when we describe the growing we are now doing as old?

Each of us has his or her own answers to the two basic questions considered in this book:

How do we maintain a sense of our own worth when the attitudes about old age in our society (and in ourselves since we've grown up in that society) are predominantly negative?

What do we need to learn which is as appropriate for our time of life as walking, talking, and learning to trust were for us when we were very young, or as mastering the three R's were when we went to school?

Maybe we will be satisfied with our answers to these questions when we find them. Maybe not. If, however, our hearts tremble somewhat as we listen to the answers we've been giving ourselves, there may be a further process of refining inside of us to be done. Especially may this be true if we examine our posture towards the unknown, for our posture on this is crucial. Is it a posture which allows us mobility and flexibility or is it crippling us unduly?

Imaginative Hospitality for an Enemy

Life after sixty is a life increasingly aware of unknowns. How can we predict the toll the aging process is going to take? More importantly, how are we going to meet it? When and how will death arrive for us? And what lies beyond the grave? Who of our peers and dear ones will precede us? Moreover, we live at a time

16

when our place in society is ambiguous, in flux, when science is making discoveries which may change what we mean by old age by extending life considerably. Very little is certain for us, socially or personally.

Unknowns, of course, have always been a part of life, but it is safe to say that the older person's feel about the unknown is unique. Not knowing for sure what is out there and beyond may, or may not, affect the younger person's immediate horizon. He feels he has some leeway. For the older person, unpredictability is integral to whatever he sees as he opens and closes the daily window. Thus, to examine how we react to this convergence of so many unknowables is an exercise of the first priority.

For those of us whose ways of relating to the unknown up to now have tended to be more of the pull-and-tug-at-it variety, so that it will more nearly fit familiar shapes and suppositions, there may be the vague feeling, as we now approach old age, that this will no longer do. The balance of power begins to feel as though it were shifting. We sense that what lies ahead may no longer be appropriated or manipulated as it has been and that budgets, health, friends, energy, cannot be counted on in quite the same old way. More and more we sense *we* will be the ones *changed*, rather than the ones doing the changing.

If one must try to alter one's way of meeting the unknown, then, what are the resources? Whatever faith one has tested and tried up to this point, surely. This faith can take the form of faith in ourselves, as we anticipate encounter with the unknown, and/or faith in

17

the unknown itself. In any unknown there is what we do not know about what others will do; and what we do not know about circumstances and chance. Most of all, though, it will be ourselves, future tense, who are the enigma. Can we count on ourselves? What will we be like in a crisis we have never known ourselves in before?

There is no way of knowing the self in advance with any absolute certainty, especially in advance of something like the closing years of life, the shape of which is not only unknown but, from the stereotypes at least, would seem to be threatening as well. We may have built up a basis for faith in ourselves over the years, but any faith, however real it may have been, always remains to be tested again and again in the future.

One of the best ways to test ourselves is to relate vicariously to the experiences of our peers. It is here that we can realistically find some of the answers, not only as to what the experience is going to be like, but what we are going to be like in it. We can reduce the unknownness a bit by inching ourselves ahead, imagining ourselves *there*. We can place ourselves, and our faith, in imagination, alongside of saying to ourselves that if that person who is so frail, if that friend who has had so many bad breaks, can face it with dignity, then perhaps we can also. If we turn our faces in the direction of what we dare to hope about ourselves, and if we are unafraid of the fact that we may fail many times as we go along, then we, too, have the makings of a durable faith—the kind that can protect us against the inroads of too much fear and the acids of disillusionment and despair.

To have faith in ourselves as we face the unknowns ahead is one thing, but we have said that faith, as a resource, could also mean faith in the unknown itself. How is this possible and why, in any case, should it merit our trust?

In *Patterns of Renewal*, Laurens Van der Post uses stories of the African Bushmen to describe vividly renewal. He contrasts the primitive world with our own and says that primitive man divides time into the knowing-period and the period-before-knowing. Primitive man regards the latter period as the best milieu for his spirit and soul, and he guards against its loss for as long as he can. Why? Because the period-before-knowing is thought of as that time and that place where the "image-making thing" in humans can be most active. It is only in this period that our sense of awe and wonder, curiosity and surprise are seen as having full rein to receive those messages which can never be fully contained in words, or conveyed in pictures and rational explanation.

But, says Van der Post, we moderns contrast strongly with primitive man. We are angry with what we do not know. We hate not knowing. And we hate finding ourselves in the period-before-knowing. We even regard the period as our enemy. One wonders. Why should we hate it? We cannot have knowledge unless there is a period before knowledge. True, we may not want to spend all of life in such a period. One can even appreciate a sense of thoughtful impatience with the time before knowing, because it is this very kind of impatience which has spurred man on to invention and scientific discovery. But when modern man wants to rid himself entirely of such a period, thinks of it as the enemy, and feels, because it is something over which he does not have complete control and domain, that it must therefore somehow be against him, this is saying more about modern man than about the unknown. Such a posture means that he is depriving himself of an enormous energy which is his natural birthright.

We who are aging can take a lesson from primitive man and his faith in the unknown. We face not only immediate and nearby unknowns. Our time of life also thrusts us directly out towards the many ultimate unknowns, whose full scope and meaning can never be packaged and neatly labelled "knowledge," yet they beckon us forward to points beyond definition and total comprehension. Our time of life should find us taking full advantage of this beckoning. The psychiatrist Dr. Otto Von Mering speaks of the three S's which characterize old age: sleeplessness, solitude, and silence. They do, indeed, increase as we grow older, and most of us dread them for it is here in these three par excellence that we experience the unknown in full measure. But we can, as well, think of these three S's as good laboratory settings which go with our time of life for the very purpose of affording us a framework where we can learn and practice imaginative hospitality for the enemy.

Hospitality for the unknown would mean letting ourselves be open to it long enough to sense its terrifying, exhilarating, stretching enormity and the magnitude of its beyond beyonds. It would also mean letting the unknown be just that. Many of us make matters worse by adding to our annoyance or anger over the unknown, our fear as well. This is, in a way, turning the unknown into a known and saying we know it's going to be bad. Otherwise, we must ask ourselves, why do we fear it? The unknown is by definition just that. We do not know. Since we do not know what lies out there ahead, beyond, around, we must live with the possibility that it can be as much a prelude to something liberating for us as restrictive; as much something beneficial and growth-producing as harmful.

Negative Expectation and Stereotypes

Another way to plumb in some depth what we mean when we say to ourselves that our current growing is old is to look at the role which expectation and stereotypes may be playing in our attitudes. We have been saying that the unknown may be made worse by negative expectation, but is old age itself made worse than it need be by our expecting it to be that way?

There is, of course, no way of our knowing for sure. It is not the kind of thing which lends itself easily to controlled experiment, but Ruth Boyer in her book *Tomorrow Is Living* points out that there are some intriguing clues. A group of doctors, psychiatrists, social workers, nurses, and aides teamed together to work with a group of elderly people who, up to that point, had been classified as hopelessly senile. Their presence and their attitudes surrounded the group of elderly with a

21

set of positive expectations and, in time, many became continent, were able to talk sensibly to others, began to care about their grooming, were able to participate in self-government and some, eventually, were even able to leave the hospital.

We can take this approach of positive expectation and move it from a group to a personal level and to a particular symptom with which we are all familiar—forgetting. Most of us think forgetting goes with old age. In other words, we expect it. We do not think it goes with youth, so we do not think twice when a young person forgets. Neither does he. Not so for us. Now that we have reached a certain age we do not forget that we forget. We notice it. And we pop it into a little pigeon hole marked, "What Goes with Old Age," thinking, "There I go again! That's what happens, I guess." If this occurs often enough, anxiety-to-panic can set in, making us, in turn, even more forgetful. It makes a difference, when we get confused and cannot remember why it was we went up to the attic, to have someone around who says, in a matter-of-fact voice, "You were going to look for that snapshot, remember?" Adding casually, either by facial expression, attitude, or words, "I forget too sometimes. We all do."

Dr. Muriel Oberleder, chief psychologist in the geriatric service of Bronx (New York) State Hospital, says that, in her experience, she has noticed a double standard in the treatment of patients who have symptoms of incontinence, confusion, regressive behavior, rambling, and disorientation, depending on what the patient's age is in the hospital chart. If the chart reads a younger person, the patient is treated, rehabilitated, and *expected* to become independent. If the chart reads an older person, his illness is treated as senility and, even if recovery occurs, he is overprotected and treated as dependent, often with institutionalization recommended.

This is not to say that senility is not a real illness or that deterioration of certain parts of the body is not an objective fact. It is to say that negative expectation may make matters worse. Often symptoms, which if they were treated early could result in cure, are allowed to go on under the assumption that they are par for the course for older people, and thus, when the person does arrive for treatment, complications may have set in and it is too late.

Moreover, negative expectations produce in all of us a certain anxiety and what is called senility may be as much a response to this as to growing old. Dr. Oberleder points out that, just as senility seems to go with old age, so certain symptoms are especially prevalent among other age groups as well—for example, bed-wetting among children and drug addiction among teen-agers. We do not say, though, that childhood causes bed-wetting or that adolescence causes addiction. Rather, we think of these more as responses to the emotional strain and stress peculiar to that age, with the implication that, if we could remove the stress and surround the age period with more positive expectation, the symptoms might be less severe.

While we cannot always regulate the expectations others may have of us, we do have something to say about the images we entertain of ourselves. Dr. Robert

Butler, research psychiatrist in the National Institute of Mental Health, reports on a study he made of what he called the use of age-defense by elderly patients who were hospitalized. What he observed repeatedly went something like this: Patient demands; staff responds because of patient's age. Patient makes more demands and, when these are not answered, falls into the "no one cares about an old man" syndrome. The overworked staff explodes. This is followed by guilt, anxiety, and renewed friendliness on both sides but with the same old set of expectations more or less intact: nurses feeling, "What can you expect? He's an old man after all"; and patient feeling that there isn't much time for a poor old man.

To quote such a study is not to say that dependency is not real or that poor old men (and women) do not need genuine help. But again, it does raise the question of how much those of us who are old (since all of us were raised in a society which expects certain things of oldness) reflect our expectations by using—perhaps, at times, even abusing—our age and thus creating more dependency in ourselves than need be there.

Positive Attitudes When Negatives Are Real

When our negative attitudes and expectations about the growing-old process are warranted, and when no amount of positive expectation can change things—in fact, when positive expectation seems like some kind of a pollyanna gimmick or even a mockery, because our worst fears are being realized—what then?

Perhaps we lose our spouse or face continuing, wracking pain. Perhaps we are experiencing increasing confinement due to an incapacity or feel the despair that goes with knowing that the outcome of something on which we have invested a lifetime will not be clear before we must go. Maybe our income has been radically altered, or some long hoped for plans have been interrupted, or the value system with which we have met a life-time seems now no longer appropriate, and we are hopelessly confused and without anchor. How can we, in any honest and consistent way, maintain a positive attitude in the face of negative realities such as these?

Yet there have been those who have done so.

Positive attitudes when people are facing severe odds are as much a matter of the human record and as real a part of our environment as negative ones. Just as we need to know the extent to which our society has instilled in us predominantly negative attitudes and expectations about growing old, so we need to be aware of those whose positive attitudes have been tried and tested in the vicissitudes that are inevitable with old age, and have survived. We can also, if we choose, do more than be aware of them. We can let those who have been where we are, and who have been able to be more positive about it than we are, be quietly present to us in our time of need.

How present to us?

When we are in despair, a person of great strength may, actually, be too much for us. Sometimes to have someone around who has done nobly, when we ourselves are a long way from so doing, may only accentuate the contrast. We need to be honest with ourselves. In that case, we seek them out not because of their nobility, impressive and challenging as that may be. Rather, we are drawn to them because they have already been through what we are now facing. They represent, therefore, someone who understands and knows well what it is like. People who know what it is like are a great comfort and a great resource. They articulate for us, in our numbness and dumbness. They do more. Absorbed as we are with the shock of our own moment they make us experience ourselves, not as someone isolated and lonely, but as part of a vast company which spans time and space.

So we call on them not to impress us with their nobility. Nor do we ask them to act as leaders, out there and ahead, telling us how to proceed. They cannot do this since they take strides, and we take small steps. Their formulas cannot solve our problems. Nor should they deprive us of our own individual destiny and responsibility. Yet they are important for us as needed companions of the way. And their positive attitude is important. It is the proof we need that it can be done, and this proof woos us to keep on exploring for our own answers beyond our false starts, our half-hearted tries, and our halfway-house stops.

The wealth of positive responses to be found, and their variety, demonstrate the fact that there is no one mold, no one perfect way to do it. We see some older people coming at the adversities of old age with a keen sense of humor and the saving light touch. Others we watch as they attack with the blunt no-nonsense kind of approach. Some hold on with a stubborn and indomitable will, others with the fantasy and imagination of the penniless old man who left a will bequeathing to all young lovers the world of beauty he remembered from his youth.

In addition to those we may already know about, there is the whole gamut of history on which to draw. People have been growing old since the beginning of time—maybe not as old as we grow today, but old at least as it was felt in their day. Even the ancients of biblical and classical times, far from appearing old-fashioned and out-of-date, are highly relevant to us in our own age. They were real people, and the problems of old age they faced were real, whether it was a Moses unable to enter his promised land or a Hecuba tearing her gray hair in grief. The basic adversities in aging are universal, and the human spirit, when it affirms, is contagious across the centuries.

Take Jeremiah, who comes alive for us through the pages of that ancient book bearing his name. In his latter years as he faced the end of a long and energetic life devoted to proclaiming the values of God, he saw all those values in jeopardy. His country was falling into the hands of the enemy; his countrymen were facing exile. At that low point he made a gesture, a symbolic gesture of hope. A piece of land in his hometown came on the market. It was, of course, of no value given the abbreviated sense of future for country and self, but Jeremiah bought the piece of property anyway. It was as though he were saying, "This land on which I have spent my whole life and which is now doomed may yet

27

be of worth at some future time and beyond my being able to see it come to pass. Trapped in my own period of unknowing, I yet opt for hope."

Or again, there are those stirring pages to be found in the *Journal* of Katherine Mansfield, who did not want to die without leaving her record that she believed suffering could be overcome. That record continues to be alive for all of us who take the trouble to read her and let her testimony be present to us. Out of her own awful and increasing pain, she could put down on paper that when one thinks, "Now I have reached bottom, now I can go no deeper," still one does go deeper. Hers were not idle words. Even if suffering was not, as she believed, a "repairing process," she kept her own fortitude in repair.

Why are we not only moved but encouraged to face our own pain when we read this woman's journal? She is a stranger whom we will never meet. Her record is of such nobility that few of us can hope to emulate it. Yet the spirit which emanates from those pages draws us to it and warms our hearts. She speaks to us wherever we may be in our round with human pain, not out of theory but knowledge, not out of conjecture but hard experience, and this makes us take a new look at our old selves. We go away from meeting up with her ready to reexamine our taken-for-granted assessment of our capabilities. How deep could we go? How strong are we? Maybe deeper and stronger than we had thought.

We began this chapter by saying that most of us do not even think about aging until suddenly something happens to make us see ourselves as aging persons. We know, then, that what is meant is we are growing old. We tried to let ourselves down into that happening in our lives in order to get the feel of it. What are some of the moods and meanings that well up in us when we think of ourselves as old? We found that, more than we may have thought, we have the exciting opportunity of choice. We literally live our closing years, and our aging weeks and days, at all sorts of crossroads. Many things are not that settled about our lives. Our freedom is real and a measure of choice will go with us right to the end.

We can choose what posture to take towards the unknown. We can reexamine our expectations about old age, since the potentials, as uncovered by research, are so challenging while the stereotypes are so limiting. And when we are in crisis, we can decide whether or not to find, for company, those who have been where we are, are able to say better than we can what it is like, and have met it positively.

CHAPTER 2

Growing Old: Challenge in a Changing Society

We have been trying to find some of the ways we feel about growing old, while raising questions about those feelings. We also live in a society which, like all societies, has certain policies and attitudes regarding old age. In our case they are predominantly negative. How do we maintain motivation to go on and to find self-respect in the doing of it under these circumstances?

Individuals have a certain amount of freedom both *within* society and *from* society. We will look at freedom from society first.

A Beyond-Society Set of Values

We find ourselves in a situation which has built into its very structure no significant place or function for the older person. Ours is also a society which gives us the freedom not to agree with it, if we so choose, and the education which enables us to criticize it intelligently. As older members of this society we may need to exercise this freedom at some point and work our way through the giddiness that goes with such an exercise. This is because American societal values do not, to use a good Quaker phrase, speak to our condition.

In the current debate among specialists in the field as to whether older people should withdraw gradually from society or remain actively engaged in it, there are some who think that the older person has more to do than to learn how to withdraw. They see an "unlearning process" as also needed. They feel that the "geriactivists" (those who urge older people to remain active and busy) often put old people at a great disadvantage by stressing values which, while they may have made America great, are of no value to the old and dying.

In any case, there comes a time when we are bound to question many American values deeply inculcated in all of us, such as mastery over nature; predictability and control over the future; work and achievement; beauty, youth, and productivity. These values must be unlearned simply because they are contradicted by waning energy, chronic illnesses, disability, and death. But we must also learn new values, and what value system is there which speaks to the universal experience of old age? Where do we go to find the basis for a sense of worth when we are nonproductive? A feeling of being attractive when our physical appearance is anything but? A sense of resiliency, grace, and dignity when we are losers on one front after another at a time when there is less opportunity to compensate for loss?

It is one thing to say that we ought to be free of society's values and quite another thing to achieve such freedom. If we have been reared in our society and are dependent on it, how can we be free of it? Are there ways? Is such freedom real and viable, so that we can live by it, or is it just a theoretical postulate? It is not something immediately apparent, but it can be found, and not as the result of a contrived pep talk either. One finds this kind of freedom, not by naïvely assuming that one has it, but by discovering wherein he or she is or is not free, so that we can more wisely use what we have and not waste time being frustrated over what we do not have. This kind of freedom from society can be gained through knowledge and through the risk of faith.

Knowledge gives us a certain edge on society and our place in it. We know, for example, that other societies treat, and have treated, their old people quite differently. To know this already gives a relativity to the way we do it here. From history we know too, that the basis on which the majority, or the strong, or the economically productive at any one point in time have given out status or popularity has not always proved to be the wisest, or even the most creative, one. Often looking back over the long range of history it is seen that individuals and groups of low status and popularity and some who are even physically weak and handicapped have nevertheless contributed a great deal to the welfare of the human race and to the meaning of life.

Knowledge about how we have acquired the attitudes we have, the values we profess, and about how we have become a self can also produce this same subtle sense of emancipation from the heavy hand of society. If we know how society controls and defines us, and in what ways we ourselves participate in this process, liberation has already set in. A puppet who knows he is a puppet is no longer just that. Knowledge like this gives us, on the intellectual level, objectivity about our society; on the emotional level, a healthy skepticism about, and a certain distance from the prevailing attitudes and controls. This does *not* mean that we are not still involved in, and vulnerable to, society. Nor does it mean that we can survive off somewhere without it. It does mean, though, that our society's definition of who we are need not be the only, or the last, word about us.

There are stimulating questions posed for us as a result of all this. Having been thrust out of our particular societal womb as it were, now where are we? Who are we? If our identity may be more than just what society says, or what society and self interacting together say, then where is that "more" to be found? Who, what is it? And is some kind of relationship possible between self and that "more" which is beyond society?

We are back to our unknowns and to the excitement of risk and the privilege of choice for again there is no way of knowing for sure. "To be human," says Peter Berger in *The Precarious Vision*, "means to live with inconclusive information on the ultimate meaning of things." To be human, then, also means there is no way of avoiding the risk involved in making some kind of an answer to what kind of a world we think this is and then living our lives on the basis of whatever answer we choose. Our answer may be explicit or implicit, but our daily choices and the feel of things will be different for each of us depending on whether we see ourselves in a universe where the forces at the heart of it are basically hostile, neutral, or supportive to the growth of human personality.

Biblical tradition says that, though we live in society and are responsible to it, it did not create or define us. It presents the image of God as the Creator and man as the one "whom God addresses." It is God, says Peter Berger, in discussing the precariousness of human identity, who "calls man out of nothingness, gives him a name, and remembers him forever." Or, put another way, it is not society's definition of our status but God's recognition which is the definitive one. In biblical tradition, God is pictured as confronting individuals, never societies, with the decision as to who they believe they are and what they think their response to him should be. It is the Eternal One confronting each person in his or her own unique condition with choice saying, "Your human identity, your authentic being and worth are beyond the particular assurance, or lack of assurance, you may receive from any human being or any society—even those on whom you count the most. Moreover, the worth of the other person must be seen by you not only in terms of what he may or may not do for society or for you, but also, and always, in terms of his worth to *me*. And that worth is infinite."

There is something both heart-warming as well as profoundly disturbing about finding oneself at the other end of this kind of a divine imperative. The Greek word for this unconditional love, this affirmation of each human being by God, is *agape*. It is not a response to a person's being worthy of love; rather, it is the creative cause that enables men and women to love themselves and others. Agape is, like our sex, skin color, and the time when we were born in history, a gift to be accepted in trust or resented and resisted, but never merited on the basis of how we function. The fact that agape is not the result of an achievement test is, perhaps, the most baffling, not to say repellent, thing about it to us moderns, trained as we are at winning our place in the scheme of things on the basis of what we *do*.

There is a special message for the aging person in agape, for there is nothing we can *do* about our age. We cannot change it. There is, however, something we can do about acceptance—acceptance not only of the givenness of our years but of God's creative affirmation and acceptance of us. Yet as Paul Tillich said, "The most difficult thing in the world to accept is acceptance."

To return, then, to our question of whether the aging person is free enough to discover, and then learn to live by, values other than those which predominate in our society—the answer is yes. There are ways for us to be free of society's view of us even while we recognize the crucial role it plays in our lives. Through knowledge, and through the risk of faith, we may experience a sense of identity beyond that which society creates in us and a sense of worth beyond the status society imposes on us.

Responses to the Label "Nonproductive"

Though the beyond-society value system we have just been discussing can make for a profound difference in a person's motivation and sense of worth, this does not alter the fact that there are many difficult givens *within* a society which we must face. All societies say, in effect, to the older generation, "Move over and make room for the oncoming generations." And, though the how and when of this varies, all societies mark this moving-over moment or process with some kind of ritual, symbol, or ceremony. In Burma, the old go off to meditate. In India, sexual life after the birth of grand-children is frowned upon. In Japan, old women change the colors in their kimonos. Here in these rites are visible reminders to individual and society alike that a new reality is to be faced.

In our society we have our own rites for moving over and our own way of noting them, retirement being among the most obvious. Our society does not need the older person in order to have an efficient and productive technology. It needs a mobile labor force. Thus, retire-ment has been institutionalized, and there are few other useful, relevant, prestigious grooves into which the re-tired person can fit.

But even though we are no longer earning a living, raising a family, or doing the world's work, there are other things to do, and our society not only tolerates but encourages pursuit of them, giving the individual wide latitude in doing so. The older person is free to start something and stop it as many times as he wants; to try out several areas, not just one, or not to try any-thing at all. Pressured as we may have been during the rat-race days, there is no government policy or public opinion to force an older person into a mold. Even if his status is peripheral and nonprestigious from the vantage point of a highly trained, fast moving, productive technology, that same status, seen from a personal, existential point of view spells considerable freedom and choice. And our society is full of individuals who have used that choice to build into their closing years useful, interesting, pleasurable, and helpful experiences.

All of this may result in older people gradually developing (quite inadvertently) a very important, necessary, and even productive role for themselves after all, namely that of teaching others how to grow old. We know that this is a time without precedent as far as the greatly increased numbers of older people are concerned. In this brand new situation many things have not yet firmed up, and it is in such times that individuals are often able to weave their own definitions of usefulness and productivity into the social fabric. There is no one whom our society presently holds responsible for teaching people how to grow old in the way, say, that it holds parents responsible for teaching children how to grow up. Will the family, the church, the government, the school, or industry teach how to grow old? But why not the old themselves? Who are better qualified to teach what it feels like, and what all the varied ways are of handling what it feels like? Who are better qualified than the old to show, by example, that in the moving-over process, the mood need not necessarily be restrictive, or the colors somber, and that, when one arrives in the new "category" one does not automatically have to delete all the active, the useful, the bright, and the funny, or turn into an ascetic. And who better qualified than the old to teach (if only by their presence) that all those younger-than-old are only kidding themselves when they think of older people as a category called "they," "over there" as though that left them "us" and "here." No one knows better than the old, who have just come through the transition and have discovered by personal experience just how self-defeating such a societally popular attitude can be, how important it is to be taught early that "the old" are only, and always, ourselves at some point in the life-span.

Breakers of the Taboo

Our society, however, conveys more to its members about old age than the need to move over because they are not productive. It also conveys a distinct distaste for old age which ranges all the way from ignoring the older segment of the population to avoidance and even open hostility.

Older people, for example, pick up a fashion magazine and, though they constitute a good percentage of the market, they rarely see themselves as models displaying clothes appropriate for them. Or a study of county hospitals is made over a period of two years, and the author concludes that when older people were admitted to the emergency service, the treatment they received, more often than not, was delayed and perfunctory. Even the ambulance driver, according to the report in David W. Sudnow's *Passing On: The Social Organization of Dying*, had made up his mind in advance what the quality of service was to be. Or a retired man was asked to take on a community leadership job, but, as Sylvia

Porter wrote in one of her columns about why people dread the retired status, he failed. Why? Because he no longer had behind him the prestige of his old job as plant manager, in urging people to cooperate.

This attitude of tending to ignore, avoid, or devalue those in old age was one of the concerns of The White House Conference On Aging, 1971, which listed a number of studies showing that, in the following professions, some form of discrimination is practiced: dentistry, social work, medicine, psychotherapy, and the ministry.

Slowly a question emerges from all this across-the-board data and then persists: Why?

In the case of the helping professions, one obvious answer is that most older people have chronic illnesses, and it is not hard to understand how difficult it must be for any well-trained professional, no matter what his or her area, to be satisfied with limited improvement. One wonders, though, if this is the total explanation. The White House Conference Report refers to several authors (Kazzaz and Vickers; Pearlman, Stotsky, and Dominick) who say that "an unconscious fear of death" may be associated with the tendency of many in the helping professions to avoid the elderly and the dying.

Older people have been referred to as "visible reminders of trouble." In primitive societies, the old were "the-about-to-die." That was the actual meaning given to the word "old." And there is a sense in which, even today, that is as accurate as it was in simpler societies. Death is becoming age-specific in the United States. There is a trend towards the localizing of death in old age so that, increasingly and in a literal sense, old people are the ones in our society to remind about death.

Could it be that the alienation felt towards the old is because, unconsciously, their presence reminds us of the fact of our own death? If this is true, the fear is present in all of us—old and young. Maybe that is why their own oldness is repellent to so many old people themselves.

There is, undoubtedly, a normal human dread of death, but it is exaggerated in our case by the taboo with which our society has surrounded it. We can be grateful that this taboo is beginning to be broken. The more older people there are and the more visible they become, the more the taboo will be challenged. Reading the new research coming out on how people in our society face death and dying and open discussion of all this material cannot help but free us of unduly morbid fears.

In the final analysis, however, the problem surrounding our fear of death cannot be solved by a challenging of taboo because of the presence in our population of an increasing number of "old." Nor can it be exorcised through rational discussion or continuing research on what constitutes mental health. The solution to fear of death (and thus, it may be in large measure to society's, and even our own, negatives about aging) lies in the lonely moments of individual choice: What is the faith we are willing to risk since we can never know for sure? Do we believe, or do we not, that death, like life, is a meaningful event? And do we believe that it is given to human beings to probe that meaning?

We began our chapter thinking about the predominantly negative attitudes towards growing old to be found all about us. We wondered how we might find continuing motivation and self-respect when a society which stresses productivity above all else labels us non-productive, and when it does not want to be reminded of the facts of life and death we represent. We found that we may gain a measure of freedom from society by bringing knowledge and faith to bear. We found, too, a certain freedom within society as well. We have time; and the job of teaching the young and the middle-aged what it means to grow old and what it means to die is still open. Thus, it may yet turn out that there is a unique, useful, and very much-needed place for us after all.

OUR PRESENT OFFERS US FRESH OPPORTUNITIES

CHAPTER 3

Kith and Kin, Good Growing Ground

For the most part, our present is a taken-for-granted performance. We tend to move along in it with well-worn, habit-set responses both in the way we perceive others as well as in the way we think they perceive us. What would happen if, rather than going on and on, keeping up with others in the same old way, we thought of our relationships as an area where something fresh, at times even novel, *might* happen because something *has* happened to us? Our oldness is what is new about us, for who of us has ever been old before? And always, when something new and different happens to a person, it offers the possibility that a change in dynamics might develop between that person and others; that a bit of growth in one will correlate with, or even spark, growth in the other. Relationships are never all set. They are moving, responsive, alive kinds of things.

Nowhere would it be more appropriate to test that responsiveness than in the family.

In the novel *Come Spring*, Ben Ames Williams draws

on the diaries kept by some quite ordinary, everyday kind of folk during the American Revolution. The story gives us a glimpse into the kind of family life where each saw the others as "good growing ground." Relationships with kith and kin offer the potential of being good growing ground for us, too. This is because, of all ties, family ones remain most important to the end. Dr. Richard A. Kalish points out that, no matter what their position on the withdraw/remain active dilemma, the majority of individuals when they do withdraw, do so *into*, not *out of*, the family.

With this much at stake, it is important for us to know what in family research during the last decade affects us. It has produced evidence both of continuity and of change. Each calls for a different kind of response from us and both have positive elements in them for us.

Marriage and Sexuality in the Later Years

To raise the question of whether there might be new ways of relating, one to the other, in an old marriage tempts one to say that if it has lasted that long, don't tamper with it. Keep hands off. It must have its own built-in formula for survival—a kind of delicate balance worked out over the years. Why talk of change or the new? Alternatives to marriage for the older couple are no longer viable; illusions about each other are no longer possible; divorce at this period is not sought. Leave the relationship alone.

Statistics about marriage in the period just before old age—that is, in the postparental, preretirement period

46

—make depressing reading. Texts and studies are full of such familiar words as "disenchantment," "devitalized," and "decline." Studies and statistics about marriages of those sixty-five years of age and over, however, (and granted that research results on these marriages is biased by the very fact of their survival) make more optimistic reading. They use a different set of words. These marriages are "stable," "calm," "serene," and "sure," and the studies are very specific about what is meant. They say that in marriage, as we grow older, we stop talking to each other about our children and begin talking about repairs and religion. They describe marriage among this group as highly conventional, and preoccupied with concerns for health—our own as well as that of our spouse. Harold Feldman of Cornell says that couples at this stage "have come to terms with their marriage."

As one reads the research, it makes marriage sound dreary to dull, with no laughter in it and barely a smile, a kind of egoism *á deux* with no distance, risk or excitement but, rather, just going through the same old familiar set of motions.

But is this the whole story? What the studies fail to convey, or perhaps cannot put into words, is how dear becomes any familiar thing in old age, but especially marriage; how dear the familiar motions—body turning in its sleep to follow, so well, the other; body in its waking hours, face lighting up; the ever so slight pucker in the brow; the look flashed; the slight amusement around the mouth; the walk, the bounce; the message inaudibly given; the tone of voice so quickly heard without anyone else in the know. So deeply implanted in us, over the years, are the cues and clues, so ready the response, so welcome the comfort, the sheer blessed comfort of "stable, calm and sure," the knowing that someone will be there and can be counted on, the relief of being able to flop down, let down, *be* down, knowing that the other knows full well this is not all there is about us.

Couples who have lived together for a very long time, and even when they do not wax enthusiastic about it, have built up real capital--riches as tangible as any money. It is comfortable to have that kind of money in the bank. One relies on it, builds on it, and is not cheated. One of the less advertised functions of marriage, as far as young lovers are concerned, yet one of the more priceless, is that of insuring against loneliness in old age.

The Beatles sing a song about a young lover who wonders if his beloved will still need and feed him by the time he is sixty-four. They need to be answered. It is *great* to be fed and needed at any age but especially at age sixty-four, seventy-four, eighty-four. However it is experienced, whether joyously, matter-of-factly, or not appreciated at all until it is taken away, one of the great pleasures in life is to have someone there, someone to call your own, to eat, laugh, cry with, to yell at, remind you, help you find your glasses, zip the zipper . . .

But how can it be? How can routine and business as usual be the bill of fare when everything about an old marriage is change? The possibility of disruption through widowhood hangs over it in a way that the divorce rate never threatened the young or the middle-aged marriage. And, as husband and wife retire, or leave the active categories, the marriage relation itself becomes something quite new and different. There are new decisions to be made as to who does what, with how much of it. A brand new relationship has to be forged now that both are free all day, often in smaller quarters, with less money.

How do people react to this change and this new period? Although there is a great deal of variety in the way they do it, the record is that, for the most part, couples adjust. The words we read in the studies edited by Matilda W. Riley and Anne Foner are "co-ordination of roles" and "shared activities." And along with doing things together, aging married couples expect, and get, a good deal of help from each other when they are sick or incapacitated.

Marriage for older people, then, seems to be more than a security check. According to the studies, it has a record of being a good living arrangement as well—a functioning team, impressive in its efficiency. He there? Then she here. One person needs? The other pitches in. For two people in old age to be able to make this much compromise and to adjust to new quantities in budgets, new amounts in space, and new qualities in roles is an excellent example of the ability to learn in late life.

Sometimes this process of having to move over and adjust to new living arrangements and new requirements from each other has important ramifications in other areas of marriage as well. We may gain further insight about the sexual aspect of our lives or we may discover hidden traits and talents in our personalities we had not realized were there. We will look at the sexual aspect first.

All of us arrive in old age with our ideas and feelings about sex having had a long history behind them. Some have never been too happy with their sexual life while others have been deeply and joyously satisfied. Some have been partially satisfied and are wistful over the partialness. Some are more afraid than anything else; or are disgusted; or have been hurt and are resentful of that. For many it has not been any one of these feelings so much as a combination of them, at various times, and in varying degrees, throughout the years.

We also have views about these attitudes of ours. Some have been able to look at their feelings and the circumstances which have produced them, and grow in understanding of themselves and their mates. In the process, they may have been able to improve their situation or, where that has not been possible, learn to accept it and go on to find satisfactions in other areas of life. Some may not have wanted to admit the whole matter to consciousness and have lived lives alienated from a whole segment of their personhood. For many it has not been a question of honesty or repression so much as lack of knowing how to proceed. They have not known how to deal with their various feelings for fear that doing so would only add an additional burden to be lived up to, and their lives were already burdened enough. Or they may have thought that talking about sex in a rational way would somehow reduce its sanctity or spontaneity and thus produce a self-consciousness in them and their partners which could be self-defeating. Maybe they did not know anyone they felt was competent enough to help them or with whom they would feel at ease even if they could locate competence.

More importantly for the older marriage, however, is the fact that most of us have arrived in it not only with set attitudes about sex but with set attitudes about sex in old age. Attitudes from Victorian times still persist in regard to the sex life of the older person which are amazing in this day of sexual liberation. Stereotypes have it that the aging male possesses little or no socially acceptable sexuality and that sexual interest is unsuitable for women much beyond middle age. Dr. Robert Butler, a Washington, D.C. psychiatrist working with older persons, says, "The average doctor does not really think sex matters in old age." Dr. Laura Singer-Magdoff, former president of the American Association of Marriage and Family Counselors, after she had concluded a talk on sexuality which she gave to older people, had a woman of seventy come up to her with tears in her eyes and say that it was the first time she had ever heard anyone discuss sex in old age as though it were a normal thing.

We pay for this head-in-the-sand position in many ways, and one of the ways is that it has undoubtedly turned the sexual needs of many older people into a problem rather than a joy. Dr. James Peterson, who began a study of old age adjustment in retirement communities in 1964, visited a psychiatrist and a psychologist working in an age-segregated community where the average age was over seventy. He asked them to name, in order, the important areas of stress of those who came to them for help. Their answers indicated that twice as many problems revolved around the sexual area as any other.

What new could be put into an old relationship in regard to the sexual experience? For one thing all of us could learn from the research which is beginning to come out. Search for the Fountain of Youth and aphrodisiacs is as old as human history. There is no sure cure, but we can learn from what facts and studies there are and be guided by them. Masters and Johnson indicate that adjusted women show no decline in the sex drive as they grow older, though they go on to point out that many women are not adjusted in the first place. They also say that while male sexual responsiveness is diminished after age sixty, they feel that part of this may be reversible. These authors claim that, if sexual expression has been maintained with regularity over the years and there is good physical health and good adjustment to the aging process itself, sexual performance may extend beyond the eightieth-year age level. It is this kind of data which may encourage many to feel freer about exploring to their own satisfaction an area which up to now has been imprisoned by public opinion in stereotypes and taboo.

Putting something new into their sexual life would, of course, depend on each individual couple—their own experience to date with sex, and their views of it in old age, as well as their ways of communicating with each other about their satisfactions and problems. But all of us have inherited society's attitude and have been affected by that inheritance. Dr. Rubin, in his book *Sexual Life After Sixty*, states that the sexless older years are a self-fulfilling prophecy. Since we have been taught to think it is going to be a certain way that only helps to make it so. We have already seen how negative expectation has affected our lives in other ways. The new here would be to challenge whatever false expectations we may have regarding sex in old age and to support a healthy attitude towards its normalcy.

Sometimes, the process of moving over and adjusting to new living arrangements and personality needs can produce fresh insights in us in another area of our lives. To our surprise we are treated to an unexpected plus about ourselves—a trait or talent we did not think we had. Maybe he moves out into the kitchen, which he had always bypassed and, far from finding it demeaning, he begins to thrive. Maybe he learns that he can care for small children and that his pleasure exceeds clumsiness; or that he can cry, or ask for help, and that, rather than feeling embarrassed or unmasculine, it is only simple human relief that comes. Maybe she has been too dependent and timid but then finds not only that she can take over and run things, when he cannot, but that she enjoys management as well.

These bonuses about ourselves may even begin to open us up so that we actually play a part in calling them forth instead of just stumbling on them. This could mean, for one couple, a regular getting away from each other for ventilation, new perspective and then a creative return, while in another marriage it could mean just the opposite, a beginning to do all kinds of things together for the first time. Maybe she tries to learn what the attraction of TV football is, or what income tax forms are all about. Maybe he agrees to attendance at a poetry course or starting a vegetable garden with her.

Learning to know ourselves and our lifetime partners beyond what we thought we knew already *can* mean, and often does mean, a time of delight. Write love poems and novels about this time. It is as near to being a second honeymoon as the life-span offers. "I've known myself all these years and I wouldn't have thought I had it in me!" That is worth a story. "Well, I've known Fred all these years and I never knew that!" *That* might be worth a book.

Of course, if we believe that change and new circumstances have a way of calling forth surprises, we must be prepared for the fact that not all surprise is delight. Sometimes it can evoke not the fun-loving and the compassionate about us but the ugly and the petty. One of the most moving stories about interesting old people, *Tell Me A Riddle* by Tillie Olsen, describes a couple who, as they sit down to discuss where they are going to live, stumble over the "stubborn, gnarled roots of a quarrel."

It was a quarrel that had reached back over their forty-seven years of marriage. Only a novel can do justice to the longing, pain, and tragic ending in which, across the whole unresolved agony of their breach, he reaches out and takes her dying hand in his.

For some, this process of making new discoveries about the loved one, so that neither one ever has the other down pat, has been going on throughout their marriage. They have welcomed change and growth, and the never being able to take the other for granted, as that which has validated their love for one another, their witness to the fact that marriage has affirmed, rather than consumed, them.

Helmut Thielicke, in *The Ethics of Sex*, points out an interesting insight in the novel *Niels Lyhne* by Jens Peter Jacobsen, where the hero Erich is puzzled by the fact that in the sexual encounter—in that moment of ecstasy which is the essence of intimacy and closeness—when he thought that he would completely possess his beloved, he discovered there was something which eluded him, something which was inaccessible. This baffling something about her was not so much a hostile or an alien thing as an intriguing one. She could not be, he realized, totally subsumed or possessed by him, simply because of her own separateness. Yet he loved her all the more for it.

It may just be that, as with the sexual act and its moments of ecstasy, so with the process of aging and its potential growth crises, aging married lovers once again must learn this fundamental truth about the other, namely, the more-than-he-or-she-is-to-me dimension. Yes, he or she may be "ours," familiar, sure, and comfortable. But not quite. For the other one always has his or her own dimensions to address himself to, his own set of unknowns to meet and this, no matter how old we grow, and even right to the end. Marriage, then, frames a paradox. The closer we draw to one another the more we know, with a certainty, the absolute separateness of the other to be respected and never transgressed.

It is a good paradox to have learned by the time we

reach where we are. Old age is, perhaps, the supreme time of framing the fact that we came into this world alone, we leave it alone, and no intermediary, no beloved, no partner, even though that person may know us better than we know ourselves—can do for us what we must yet do on our own.

While marriage for older people can be and is a form of security, a practical living arrangement, and a time to set in motion new discoveries about ourselves, it can be much more. It can be a training ground for love, love's comforts, love's vulnerabilities, love's requirements. In marriage one tends to see the other as a person-in-relation-to-the-self. There is another dimension, though, in which to see and to hold the other. Dietrich Bonhoeffer writing in his *Letters from Prison*, and as he said, speaking "plainly," wondered how one could long for the transcendent while he was in his wife's arms. There was no point, as he saw it, for anyone to long for the transcendent under those circumstances, for that was where you already were. "We ought to find and love God," he wrote, "in what he actually gives us."

If, in marriage, one also sees the other in-relation-to-the-Creator of this vast, mysterious, but nonetheless individually felt, process of life and love, then *this* dimension cannot help but keep the closed-in, ingrown, satisfied, routine-like intimacy which marriage often produces open to that beyond itself. It is love which prevents the security marriage gives from crippling us. It is love which turns the practical living arrangement marriage affords us into something of an art. It is love which, in view of the potential for surprise and the uneven rate of growth and change, holds the couple together across the gap which growth produces in one person while the other catches up. And it is love, learned and well practiced in marriage, which will sustain and give new life to the bereaved one when aging marriage is broken.

Caring About *vs. Care* of *Aged Parents*

We have said that research data help us in understanding change and in spotting new areas for growth in marriage. This is also true for the larger family as well, as for example, between children and their aging parents. The basic issue here is: Who cares for whom? How much? And in what way? Roughly speaking, government and industry underwrite the economic support of the older person, along with his own contributions, while family gives affection and concern. A new, and as yet little known fact, may alter this pattern of the family's contribution and that is the existence, on a substantial scale and for the first time in the history of human societies, of four-generation families. We now mean by the word "family" two more or less independent groupings of two generations each—the middle-aged with their young, and the older with the very frail. This greatly complicates the issue of loyalty, responsibility, and the ability to maintain contact and keep in touch. Now, and increasingly with the four generation phenomenon, the middle-aged couple, involved in raising their still dependent young, face the question of how they can relate meaningfully and practically to the increasing dependency of both sets of their aging parents, who in turn, may have *their* parents' care.

Even more poignant is the issue from the vantage point of the fifty- to sixty-year-old woman who is caring for her frail, eighty-year-old mother. Caught in the middle of old norms (her mother fully expects care) and new emerging norms (in which people do not expect anything fully), where should her loyalty, obligation, and energy lie? More importantly for her, if she devotes all her time and resources to the frail mother, can she expect the same kind of help on the part of those younger when her time comes?

All of this means that, with individuals and couples facing such a smorgasbord of conflicting expectations, no matter which way choice goes there is bound to be considerable guilt and regret, if not open hostility. Perhaps it is here those of us who are growing older and looking for new input into old familiar relations should direct our attention.

We need to go back a bit and examine how we have conceived of being grown-up. We have been taught that this occurs when the individual moves from adolescence into young adulthood. The images we use are those of *leaving* the nest, *untying* apron strings, *freeing* oneself of the parent. All these imply a facing away from, a going in the opposite direction. Likewise for the parent. We have heard that the best parents are those who work themselves out of a job, who have learned to let go, who can face the empty nest stage and turn around to lead their own lives. Thus, maturity, which is the goal of our growing-up process, has been pictured as a state where both the child (free of the authority of the parent), and the parent (free of possessive, protective overinvolvement with the child), have turned away from each other, intent on the task of establishing their own autonomy.

But what is so valid about emancipation per se? And why stop there? Why should not the goal of growing-up be to go beyond both childish dependence and young adult independence to the establishing of an inter-adult interdependence? Yet at what point does the old concept of maturity envisage parent and grown child turning around and looking at each other all over again, this time as very special and significant adults who are authentic in their own right and who, possibly, might turn out to be quite interesting and lovable as well? The old concept never made that stage and that opportunity quite clear.

Possibilities are infinite however, in a relationship in which the older parent begins to see an adult child with fresh eyes—no longer as a projection, or a problem—in fact, not necessarily as a problem-free adult at all (for who is?) but as someone, fully grown, whom the parent has let go long enough that he can now relate to him just as he is.

There are also great possibilities in a relationship in which the adult child comes at his parent, perhaps fully and for the first time, as a person with his or her own separate life history. Long before the child existed there was a human being on the scene being shaped and shaping. Most children, no matter how old, find it difficult to conceive of their parents as distinct from the relationship they bear to them. Yet to see them as distinct individuals may lead to discovering a brand new person who has his own commitment to life and his own deadlines to meet.

What kind of things might happen in a relationship where people, already familiar as kin, yet come at one another with fresh eyes? Perhaps from the vantage point of two freed adults, and years later, some tough or delicate moments in the earlier years could be recaptured, helping each to see how the other saw and felt about it way back there.

"Do you remember?"

"Yes, of course I remember. Why were you like that? What was eating you?"

"I needed to test myself. Does that make sense?"

"I never understood you. There was one period . . ."

"Will I ever forget it! How you used to make me . . . ! How I hated that, and how I hated you!"

"I guess I was afraid if I didn't make you do all those things I wouldn't be a good parent."

"I was afraid, too. I worried about being one of the gang. What's so funny is that now I'm a parent the shoe's on the other foot."

"I guess, now that I think about it, you threatened us."

"Me threaten you? I never knew that. Never knew that you and Mom ever had any questions about raising me. It all seemed so sure."

"Well, there were times when we weren't sure . . ."

"I should know. I'm not sure we're doing the right thing half the time with our kids."

"You didn't turn out so bad."

"Well, turn that one around. Sometimes I wonder how you and Mom ever did it."

How would this kind of comparing notes, this willingness to be frank, *caring* enough to be frank—how would this kind of openness work out as the two emancipated adult generations moved into the period when the aged parent would be facing dependency?

Filial responsibility for older parents usually has not been explicitly taught or discussed in the family so much as it has been passed on by one generation to the next, in a set of implicit assumptions and in a kind of one-way flow. Today, given rapid change, filial responsibility and aged parental responsibility ought to come under the classification of continuing education in which both generations can find out if their expectations of each other jibe.

Of course, all any of us can be responsible for in the final analysis, in a two-way relationship, is our own side. Nevertheless, what we do and the attitudes we take always have an effect on the other side. If older parents need dependably responsive adult children (and they do), then adult children also need responsibly dependent aging parents. Just exactly what updated expectations and mutual rapport and responsibility between aged parent and adult child might mean in terms of the specific decisions they face as to housing, costs, and amount of aid and contact would depend on individual family circumstances. It could mean the adult child would be better able to feel inside himself or herself, as well as to say, that he still loved and cared even if a particular decision might have to go against the parent's preference.

Also, the older person would be increasingly freed to accept his growing dependence as natural and appropriate and not something which he had to hide, or for which he had to apologize. He could have what might be called a hold-your-head-high kind of dependence. This is not a contradiction in terms. With head high, what had to be done about the growing dependence could be tackled on its merits. But the shame-blame-guilt syndrome, which only complicates our feelings about dependency, by encouraging self-pity on the one hand and resentment on the other, could be eliminated.

In fact, head high, the older person might even turn out to be the key helper in getting everyone in the family to accept the reality of dependence in old age as a fact of life. Recently, *The New York Times* carried a book review of a story written for children, Rose Blue's *Grandma Didn't Wave Back*. The story is about a little girl named Debbie who is watching her grandmother become senile—a grandmother whom she loves dearly and with whom she has shared many special things. After the family discussion and decision as to what they must do, the day inevitably arrives when Grandma is to be sent to a nursing home. The review then made this significant remark, "It is Grandma, herself, who helps Debbie to accept this, and go on to grow and live."

Grandma had the hold-your-head-high kind of dependence. Out of the fact of her oldness she had found something brand new to put into a familiar relationship.

Kindred Spirits as Kin

We have been talking about marriage and older parents and their adult children, but change in family living, between the sexes and between the generations, has gone way beyond these two sets of relationships. Older people are involved in this total change in at least two ways. Their own younger kin may define their obligations to them differently, feeling that blood ties must be merited, as well as inherited, to hold. We may also expect that some from among our peers, both out of their own need and in response to the general mood of experiment in society, will gradually make new definitions themselves. This will be new, when it happens, and it will call for something new from all of us.

Being open to those in our own generation who, for one reason or another, are caught up in an experimental mood, is more difficult than being open with those younger. The behavior of those our own age challenges and threatens us far more. Yet being open to those who may want to change does not necessarily mean that we ourselves have to change. It does involve, however, our recognizing that change affects people differently.

Change in family living has come about, not only in our society, but elsewhere, because new facts have created new problems and new opportunities. These facts are as true for some older people as for some younger. Many over sixty-five have never married, or are divorced. When they live in a society which assumes that "family" is the institution to give emotional support in old age, they face a problem. Moreover, even if older

63

people do have kin ties and can count on family, what intimacy it gives must often be at a distance. Family support, however real and tangible by way of exchange of goods and services, phone calls, letters and visits, is often not close enough or daily enough to satisfy the increasing needs of the older person for contact and assistance. What is true of family is often true of friends as well. The older person faces loss here too. Drs. E. W. Busse and Eric Pfeiffer quote one woman as saying, "All of my friends have gone either to heaven or Miami Beach."

Another fact which is producing problems is the over-supply of women among the elderly, and there is no sign that this imbalance in the sex ratio is going to abate. In 1970, there were four widows for every widower. This imbalance is matched by the fact that there is an ever increasing number of younger women who continue to shoulder by themselves the dual role of home-making and working outside the home. They have their counterpart in the growing number of older women who find themselves on the periphery (both occupation-wise and familywise) and want somehow, to some extent, to be integrated back into the mainstream.

As more traditional forms of the family fail adequately to resolve some of the poignant dilemmas inherent in these facts, change is bound to come. What kind of change? According to Dr. Rose M. Somerville, older people are not welcome in such nontraditional family forms as communes. Probably change in our generation will not be as deliberate and self-conscious as in the younger generations. It is more likely to emerge because some older people have found a chance to try out something they have always had a yen for but have never had the opportunity to try. It will probably be more that it just happens to happen, and then, because it answers a need, the individuals involved decide to perpetuate it, very much like the woman, well along in years, pictured in a cartoon recently, who was on her way down a back street to the Senior Citizen Center. She had just passed, en route, a long-haired young jogger going in the opposite direction. As she watches him disappear, she thinks, "Well, why not? What's there to lose?" and off she goes thumping out her own version of jogging.

An example of the "Well why not? What's there to lose? And besides, it might just suit me" mood is seen in a new family form called "the affiliated family."

One actual case history will illustrate why even though the kin in it are adopted and not blood relatives, it still feels like family to those in it. Two women, one forty-one years old, divorced and with five children, and the other over sixty, also divorced, met and became friends because both of them were in the same church. The younger woman obviously needed help with housework and her growing children since her job took her away from the house all day. The older woman needed to earn her way and wanted to be part of a small, intimate daily group. Both needed someone to talk to and to care. They decided, after careful assessment and thought, to live together. The relationship which has developed out of this decision, say the authors, has proven to be much more than a mutually profitable exchange. It has in it some of the elements that go into the traditional family form: not only daily contact and shared income but a willingness on the part of all to make some kind of commitment to each other. The form is flexible enough to include people of various ages and can be adopted to meet a variety of personal situations.

The affiliated family is obviously not for everyone. Nor do the authors of these studies, Sylvia Clavan and Ethel Vattar, see it as in any way seriously challenging the traditional family. But for some people such a voluntary arrangement, with a loving human commitment in it, is better than living in an institution. Perhaps it is better to give individuals options rather than expecting the problem of care, contact, and intimacy to be solved exclusively by creating institutions and the bureaucratic red tape which often goes with them.

The two women, ages forty-one and over sixty, who make up such a new "family" grouping do not live in a vacuum, and what their peers think of them is important. Those of us who are part of this older woman's generation will have to decide, as will younger people, what, if any, new approach we may want to take in regard to people whose lives may have led them into forms and patterns different from our own.

CHAPTER 4

Friends and Strangers— New Input, New Output

We come now, in our discussion of fresh opportunities to be found in old relationships, to those with our own generation and with those younger.

Gray Hair and Gray Hair

The most practical question we face, in regard to relationships with our own age group can be put quite simply: Should we spend most of our time with them or should we make a conscious effort to relate to, and mix with, people younger than ourselves? If the latter, in what way?—In our housing and neighborhood? In our activities and programs? In the choices we make of companions and friends?

Research data say most of us will be age-segregated. Not quite, however. Since we prefer family first, as long as we are in touch with it in some way, we are bound to be exposed to, and in learning contact with, the several generations represented in it. But after family, statistics show that older people prefer their own age group. Not only older people have this preference—everyone does. Our society encourages age-grading. Children prefer children, college students, college students. They see each other in school and after school. Middle-aged families live together in suburbs and see mostly one another. And now, with increased longevity giving older people more and more of their peers, it is natural, in our society, for them to seek out one another and to congregate together.

Age-grading is not only a way of "placing" people by giving them a sense of who they are and how important they are vis-à-vis others. Since it is a way of life in our society, it tends to perpetuate itself by creating those very attitudes which make people want it. We grow up mixing with, and thus feeling comfortable with, those who start from the same starting points, know the same landmarks. On the other hand, we are uncomfortable with those who do not know what we are talking about. "Chicken Little? Who's that?" or, "Moses? He was a sculptor, wasn't he?" blandly asks a youngster or young person, sending the old person scuttling off, sputtering and incredulous. And likewise, there are probably a fair number of older people who are not altogether clear on the new meanings to old words like "gay," "grass," "square," and "hip," "dig it," and "cool it."

The differences go far beyond vocabulary, symptomatic as that is. Studies show that our age determines how we consume and use our leisure, what we think about religion, politics, and rearing children, and, above all, how we relate socially. So it is understandable and natural, reared as we have been, for gray hair to prefer gray hair. But do studies tell us anything about the effect on older people of spending time with their own peers?

For example, in a situation where those living together range in age from fifty to seventy, do those in their fifties move more rapidly towards feeling and acting old because of the daily contact with those older? Or do they, on the other hand, gain out of the daily encounter by being able to visualize more realistically, rather than exaggerate and fantasize, what the problems and opportunities are which lie ahead? Do those in their sixties and seventies, in turn, become depressed because of the competition and comparison with those younger, or does the presence of those in their fifties and sixties give comfort by insuring some continuity of friendship for them?

Just to ask questions like these is to point up how much the input of individual attitude and temperament can determine result. Maybe that is why there is, to date, so little research which gives us clues definitive enough to help us when it comes to making decisions. Meanwhile, generally speaking, practitioners who work with older people think it is crucial to urge them to age-mix, as they feel this is the key to remaining a part of the mainstream of life. Social *theorists*, on the other hand, disagree. They think that, given our particular society, to put older people in with those younger can only serve to increase their sense of isolation and of being on the sidelines.

To take an example, a church may decide, instead of having a special place and a special program for its older members, to keep its total program un-age-segregated and open to all. But, say the theorists, the way it works out is that older people, for a variety of reasons, are unable to participate fully in such programs and are either left out or drop out themselves. Therefore, if older people cannot walk up steps, or stay up at night, or hear and see when they get there, isn't it better, they ask, to design a program which takes some of the disabilities of old age into account?

The question becomes a more difficult one when we move from designing programs to the matter of housing. Several studies show, for example, that older people who live in a situation where others are the same age, make more friends and have a better morale because they live in a way that helps them begin to adjust to old age; they are also spared competition with the young, plus possible conflict over life-styles. On the other hand, there has been an interesting experiment in the opposite direction —one on the edge of a university campus where dormitories for students are built adjacent to a public housing facility for older people. Both age groups have been encouraged to help each other and to see each other in a number of ways. A preliminary assessment would indicate that the project has helped to reduce stereotypes held by both ages, and some meaningful contacts between the generations have been established. Whether these contacts will continue as the students move on and the old become disabled is a question researchers will want to follow.

We have yet to experiment in this country to any appreciable degree with the European plan of separate living quarters for the elderly which are placed within walking distance from, as well as within sight of, other age groups, particularly children.

Since research on the effects of living with our own age group is not definitive enough as yet, and since practitioners and theorists do not agree, the individual is going to have to make up his or her own mind. For most of us, pocketbook and health will be the determining factors rather than a conscious decision based on the findings of scholarship.

No matter which way our decision goes, however, there is the possibility of fresh opportunities for us. For one thing, there are always those, even in our own age group, who are quite different from us. A retired minister chooses to stay by his church, in a neighborhood considered deteriorating by real estate standards, and to go on ministering to the old people in it, many of whom come from a very different background from his own. A healthy woman in a retirement village spends a good deal of time with the sick in the village infirmary. An elderly woman in her mid-seventies in a low-cost housing unit volunteers in a project to search and find the isolated elderly in some of the other units near her own. The volunteer is black. Many of those she "finds" are white. One day, the volunteer is given short shrift by an elderly white lady huddled up in the corner who, though her door is ajar, makes it clear she does not want anyone to interfere with her loneliness, much less someone black. The volunteer decides not to take the rejection personally so she continues to call out a cheery hello as she passes by the open door. There was never any response until one day a voice calls out to come in, and a hand waves somewhat imperiously in order to cover up the shaking and fright. "I have to go to the hospital," snaps the white lady. "I want you to go with me."

The possibilities are there, then, of finding individuals within our own age group who are different enough from ourselves, and we from them, that we can stretch our horizons and keep from becoming parochial and ingrown.

Gray Hair and Pigtails

Julietta Arthur in her book *Retire to Action* quotes a youngster in the Foster Grandparent Program as saying, "Grandmas don't have to do anything except be there. ... When they read to us, they don't skip words or mind if it is the same story again. Everybody should try to have a grandmother . . . because grandmas are the only grownups who have got time . . . ."

Here is unconditional endorsement—a statement that we are needed and wanted from an authentic source—a group that matters. The little girl even goes on to say that we do not have to be smart to be acceptable. All we have to do is to answer questions like why dogs hate cats and have enough sense not to talk baby talk since no one understands it anyway. Well, we can do that, and we are encouraged in the doing of it by this child's obvious lack of embarrassment in saying what she likes about us.

But being a grandparent today is not what it used to be. Over the river and through the woods to Grandmother's house we go is a delightful image, especially if one pictures grandma, apron on, a cookie jar full of homemade goodies behind her and grandfather stomping into the kitchen on his way to the wood stove, his arms full of logs he has just cut from his own timber. It is an image, though, which no longer describes fact. Seventy percent of older people are urbanized; grandparenting is a middle-aged phenomenon; grandmothers no longer have to have gray hair; and many grandmothers work full time. The grandparent role, when it functions, has become an essentially maternal and nurturant one for both men and women.

It seems evident that, of all the relationships in the extended family, that of valued grandparent is not an automatically prescribed status but is one which involves personal qualities and personal intent. Not all older people want to, or can, relate happily to their grandchildren; not all grandchildren would welcome it if they could. One third of a group interviewed said they had trouble with today's grandparent role. Some did not like to think of themselves as grandparents, because they felt the term aged them. Some said they had no time for grandparenting. Others had conflict with the parents over the way the children were being raised and so chose to drop out of regular contact. Two-thirds, on the other hand, liked the idea of being a grandparent. Along with their liking, though, went certain unvoiced but definitely felt expectations. These older people were investing high hopes in the future, both in terms of what the grandchildren might achieve and also in terms of the affection their grandchildren would offer them later on.

The rewards are enormous on both sides when a relationship between grandparent and grandchild does exist, but this research points out an important clue on how to insure the rewards. We must enter into relationship with children putting no conditional clauses on our affection. We are no different than anyone else, and like everyone else we must be prepared for disenchantment. When the growing pains of adolescence come, the need to break away from home can include grandparents as well as parents. Existential living, however, becomes old age, as it does children. This means that the chance to make that wonderful, spontaneous entry into each other's world is constantly open to us. We are not responsible for our grandchildren's achievements or their discipline. We cannot dictate their future. We can enter into their present with them unconditionally if they will let us.

One of the reasons the grandparent-grandchild relationship offers so much potential is that so many of the positives in it are unique. We knew the child's Daddy or Mommie when the latter was young as the child is now. We can, better than anyone else, help the child to picture his parent as a human being who did not just arrive on the scene full blown, but as someone who had to grow and who also had to work at it, just as the child is now doing. How to talk about "when Johnny was young" is an individual matter. One does not do it, in this case, to undercut the authority of the parent, or to endlessly rehearse famous family tidbits, usually garbled. Given a certain touch, however, in the way it is done the presence of a living witness to the fact that Daddy and Mommie were also young and vulnerable, naughty and good, can add an element of realism (often delightful) to the family circle.

We add another unique dimension to the child's world. We are old. The child needs to learn what being an old person means, as well as what being a child, and being a grown-up means. And who better to teach him that wrinkles, poor eyesight, and uncertain joints are what he too can eventually expect than someone who loves him and whom he loves?

The child goes to the curb, stops carefully to ponder what he has been taught, then dashes across the street. The older person, also, is beginning to treat curbs and street-crossings with a new respect as though he, too, may have to learn a few new tricks. Watching cracks in the sidewalk may be something of a game for kids; it is a matter of survival for the old. Since both generations have some of these new learning experiences in common, they have something on which they can compare notes. And comparing notes may help the child to realize, stretching now across two generations, that grandparents, also, did not arrive full blown and that learning goes on forever.

It is not only the child's world but our own that is enriched when gray hair and pigtails get together. Children are our lifeline to a changing world, and sometimes we need them to take us by the hand as we are introduced to it. "I like language. I need more words," said a four-year-old to her grandmother one day by way of edging up on the idea that she wanted to go to the children's library. "Well, I could use a few new ones myself," said the grandmother, "so let's go together."

To accompany a youngster to a children's library and to wander around the shelves watching what he or she picks out as well as doing some scanning on our own is an eye-opening experience. Even more instructive, if one is given the opportunity, is to go home and enjoy some of the library books and records together with the child. The world we enter is not that of the Mother Goose and Aesop's Fables of our childhood, though the old favorites still abound and are loved.

Children's books today tend to reflect back to them their world, and thus they move us into areas we may not have thought of as either appropriate or interesting for young children—death and divorce, poverty, prejudice, masculine and feminine roles, pollution. Two little boys go up and down nine tenement floors (and we go with them) listening to what is happening in each apartment and getting a rather raw view of life while trying to find the blind, mouth organ player. A small girl who lives alone with her grannie hears from neighbors that the old woman, a welfare recipient, has been taken to the hospital. We go with the child as she tries to find her. A child's parents are divorced, and she is full of fear and fantasy as she asks first her mother, and then her father, what it means. In some stories, little boys play with dolls and feel all right about crying; fathers change diapers and help with the laundry and mothers work all day, to come home as tired as daddys.

Though one might think of some of these children's books as strong on a social message, there is nothing didactic or propagandistic about them. Seldom do we find a moral tacked on, or the dramatic wind-up of "and so they lived happily ever after" which we remember. Mostly, there is just period—no embroidery, folderol, or summary—rather, a matter-of-fact here's how it is. If there should be anything remotely resembling the old crescendo we knew as children, it is more apt to come out as "so they were married and lived together happily for quite some time," or even, "they enjoyed each other but decided marriage was not their life-style."

Thus we enter the child's world. Even though at times we may lift our eyebrows, and we do, as long as we have our glasses on no one will see us. That may be all to the good. It is still our world too. If we find it tough sometimes, in making an adjustment to it, it may be just as well that we keep this to ourselves.

One of the best changes in grandparent status today is that one can still be a "grandparent" even if one does not have any kin, or if one's own grandchildren are at a distance. The Foster Grandparent program has institutionalized the grandparent role and has been highly successful in giving useful and paid jobs to some older people in orphanages, hospitals, and in certain schools. But what Foster Grandparents offer need not be confined to that group. Every neighborhood and every church or synagogue must have some young parents who would appreciate an elderly member—preferably one whom their children knows—volunteering as occasional baby-sitter. If we want to relate to children—and even if we feel we can do it only occasionally—the opportunities are usually there somewhere.

Gray Hair and Long Hair

It is much more subtle and difficult for older people to relate to teen-agers and college-age young people than it is to relate to children. On the whole, older people still really do know a few things children do not. Besides, children have plenty of time to give to the relationship and are not so dedicated to their peers that they must worry about what it would be like to be seen with us. And if older people genuinely enjoy children, youngsters are rather quick in sensing the sympatico and responding to it without inhibition. Little of this is true for the teen-ager, or the college-age student. The way they spend their time is fairly well standardized in order to make them acceptable to their peers. Whom they are seen with is crucial. We also know they do not want from older people their knowledge, which is dated; their moral code, which they do not accept; nor treatises on the way the older generation has tried to solve the world's problems, since they are not impressed.

The question arises therefore: Is it possible for an older person to hope to build and maintain over a period of time any kind of honest, open, and substantive relationship with a young person today? And even if he can, would not the young person be suspect by his peers?

But many older people want to relate to young people. As one eighty-year-old woman put it, having watched several high school generations pour across her backyard every afternoon, "I'd like to talk with some of them—find out what's going on in their minds—tell them what's going on in mine. I haven't a notion though of how to

78

go about it!" Or as an older man said, "I have things I want to pass on to young people. I want to tell them some of the things that, in my humble experience, I've learned out of life. I know there's no room for dogma or orthodoxy today, but there ought to be as much room for my opinion, beliefs, and experience as there is for some of the other things they read about and hear."

If older people have some things they want to say—and this is so for most of us—then the question is: How do we do it so that we are heard? We cannot relate to a generation if there is no one in it wanting to relate to us. We cannot give, if no one wants what we have to offer. And then there is the matter, even before our learning how to say effectively what it is we want to say, of how to establish contact. Earlier, and in other societies, contact was made at the convenience of the elderly. Time with them and attention from them was something coveted by all, especially young people. Today, with the old no longer gatekeepers to such things as jobs, ownership of land, political control; with family approval and prestige no longer necessary for success, there are, in our society, no structural, built-in points of contact, no regularly appointed times for meeting between the young and the old. Family ties may bring them together, but such meetings are optional and depend primarily upon the emotional rapport of the individuals involved. In any case, mobility and often the health of older people can mean such meetings will not be frequent.

We ourselves often compound the problem by our ambivalence and ignorance, understandable as they both may be. Young people today stir up much anxiety in us. Even though we are no longer their parents, and thus responsible for them, we cannot let them be quite *that* different from us. In theory, of course, we believe that people ought to be able to relate to other human beings, and enjoy them without having to agree on all their economic and political views and religious or philosophical convictions. In theory, too, we believe that every generation has the right to intellectual integrity and freedom of thought. We not only mouth this; it is an integral—and even sacred—part of our own generation's creed, and we believe it. Nor are we in any way prepared to give up this theory or to compromise it. But then, we meet the young coming at us with bare feet, asking if they can sleep together in their parents' guests rooms, talking to gurus, and responding to music which we call noise. We forget theory and think only of getting out the soap and the Ten Commandments.

This mood of wanting to scrub and lecture however is only one part of our general stance and feeling. Not only do we have convictions about the rights of *all individuals* to change—we know that *we ourselves* need to change and grow, if we are going to keep up with things. We want to feel about ourselves, even if we are getting old, that we are not thereby going to become frozen into a position once and for all. Life is radically changing all about us, and we do not want to be shoved off on the sidelines. We know that we not only want, but need, the new ideas, the stimulus and the verve which would inevitably be the by-product of regular contact with young people.

So, we want to remain "with it," to put it in the jargon of the day. But how? That is the question. For if young people are as they are, we are as we are, too, and we cannot, at our age, not be. Nor would we be of any worth to young people, or to ourselves, if we were to "put on" something. Young people are the first to detect and reject phoniness. As for ourselves, our own integrity and honesty are crucial for us. And here we are, having been reared to wear shoes, to say thank you, to work hard, to believe that marriage is sacred, and we were reared, too, to think that these values were basic.

No. That is not quite saying it. It is more than our thinking these values are important. We have based our whole lives on them. We have invested *ourselves* in them so that they seem to be a part of our lifeblood. When they are attacked or ridiculed, we feel it is we who are being aggressed against. Since we have not only inherited but chosen many of our values as we have gone along, in a sense this is true.

All of this is complicated by a very simple human factor that occasionally breaks through. Sometimes we find ourselves talking directly with just one young person, rather than talking in general about "young people today." Sometimes, too, in that kind of situation, we see, in that young person, behind the superficial differences of hair style and vocabulary, and the even more basic difference of life-style, the kid we once were ourselves—trying things on for size, not sure, wondering, longing, hopelessly confused, not ready to make some decisions, but having to make them anyway. And we sense, in such a moment, how much tougher the choices are in today's growing-up world than they were when we were there.

One perceptive young one was quoted as saying to an older person who was about to launch into a judgment scene, "I guess what's wrong with me is that I'm the kind of teen-ager my parents don't want me to associate with." The older person, moved by the baffled look on the young person's face, let go the judgment and, for the first time, let himself down a bit into what it must be like to be a teen-ager today. "Tell me about it," he said.

What makes our moves toward the young so jerky, then, is that we want them, and need them, to be just as they are (for it is only as they are that they are the bridge for us to the world as it is); but we must also be as *we* are, or else we are of no worth to them or to ourselves. So can ever the twain really meet? And what do we talk about even if we can establish contact? Do we argue about the difference? Bypass it? Is there an alternative?

While we know we cannot give them our knowledge, authority, or set of values, we do have one thing which is not only unique but may be of some worth, especially if we ourselves regard it with all due modesty. That is our survival kit.

For a young person who is standing at the beginning and looking down the long trail, it just might be that there would be some things in that kit of enough immediacy and interest to whet his curiosity. "You mean that you've lived with the same person for forty years, and you still like living together? How is that possible? You mean you stayed on a job even when it didn't express you and you didn't like it? Why? How come you have gone so far on so little schooling? Where did you get your dignity and durability after all the prejudice you've faced? You mean you'd still have children, if you had to choose all over again, after all the hassle and expense you've had in raising us? And that life has been worth it even if you haven't always been able to explain to yourself, to your full satisfaction, just what it's all about?"

Having witnessed the arrival both of airplane and computer, Freud and the pill; having lived at the close of an industrial society and the beginning of a technological one, we have not only survived, we have survived radical change.

"Yes, but not anywhere near as radical as we face today," counters the young person. "For instance, did you ever think the end of the world was near? Or that the world would be plunged into something for which there were literally no answers?"

"Yes, as a matter of fact, we did. Several times. But looking back, change has not meant the end of the world; only the end of the world as we knew it up to that point."

Whether *the way* some human beings have survived turns out to be helpful to the young or not, there still may be a kind of simple reassurance for them in being reminded that people have lived through radical change, are still here, are able to talk about it, think back on it, and even philosophize about it as they try to make sense out of it.

One of the most important and obvious things about us, yet one of the things we often fail to take advantage of, since we seem to keep forgetting it, is the fact that we are no longer the parents of young people. We once were, but though we have now moved past that, so deeply set in us are the responses and cues, the worries, the furrowed brows, the heavy sense of responsibility that all too frequently we act like we were back there when law and public opinion held us to account. Yet we must remind ourselves that this is no longer true for us. Our position now is that of being one step removed from where the heat is, and it is this position which may be the very thing to help us bring to the situation ingredients for a new kind of relationship, namely, a less judgmental approach and a less uptight frame of mind.

What are older people to young people, if the former are no longer held by law and public opinion responsible for the upbringing, support, and behavior of the young? Both old and young are on the fringe, with some leisure time at their disposal, since they are not employed full time. This, then, leaves both free to explore nonfunctional, human qualities vis-à-vis each other.

If only we could convey to one another, across the gulf that our age-graded society has instilled in us, that neither old nor young has "arrived" and that the word "finished" does not become the human condition, no matter what the age, then perhaps we might not only reach one another but have something of enduring worth to say to one another. In this topsy turvy world of kaleidoscopic change perhaps we could learn the simple but evidently difficult business of just "being there" to one another, as the little girl in the Foster Grandparent program said.

What would "being there" mean? Not having the same drive as their parents to make things clear, perhaps we could learn to listen more? A young person in trouble with the law, with a girl friend or boyfriend, with parents, or with the school authorities needs a place to take such concerns. Others may want to talk about the fact that they do not know what to do for a living; do not even know what living is for, for that matter. But they do not want answers. They want to be able to articulate their feelings on their way to their own answers. In doing this, they do not want to think out loud before a judgment seat, or within hearing distance of a voice of authority; or, more subtly, before someone whose own reputation and interests are still heavily involved in what they decide. Yet there is no point in talking into a machine or a computer. They just need someone, very human, who respects the fact that here is an emerging individual in need of someone who is willing to listen as intelligently and as quietly as he or she can.

A student writes to a retired professor whom she had known earlier in college, both in class and outside of class. The student had been in an automobile accident and has been disfigured and disabled for life. "Shall I live?" asks her letter. "Tell me why. I don't know anyone else to write to. I've been out of touch with my parents ever since college, and you've lived long enough. You ought to know."

What can the older woman say to the younger one? She has no proof for her reasons as to why she votes for life. She has never been where this young woman is. She is not being asked to live with disfigurement and disability. Moreover, the professor is not without her own problems and doubts. Yet she cares for the girl and for the girl's continuing to live. She communicates this and is heard.

It is not for-sure answers or over-all solutions that we can give one another. We do not have them to give, no matter what our age. What we can offer is our caring and concerned presence.

A young teen-ager came home and flung herself on the bed in despair. Her boyfriend had gone on drugs. They had had a fight over it and she had lost. The grandmother was alone in the house when the girl came home. The grandmother said nothing in words, but she said a good deal by her posture, her touch, her look, and by her quiet going about business as usual until the grief and hysteria had subsided. Whatever she might have to say could wait. Months later, the granddaughter said in a casual offhand way, "You'll never know how glad I was you didn't say anything on that day. Or how glad I was someone like you was in the house when I got there."

In Ann Head's novel *Mr. and Mrs. Bo Jo Jones,* the story of a marriage of necessity between two high school students from widely different backgrounds, the grandmother of the girl manages to keep her own integrity and her views; she does not override the parents, who are already alienated from their daughter, yet she conveys to the couple that she is for them. The older woman provides an indispensable point of reference—an honest, unsentimental, even testy, yet genuinely interested, presence for them to turn to in their need.

Can we do this kind of being there? Maybe we can and maybe we cannot. Being a sincere and keenly involved listener is halfway between the social activist's position and that of the objective observer. It is a posture that fits older people well, since many of us are not trained in the latter and do not have enough energy or mobility for the former. It is not without its own requirement of courage and risk-taking though. And imagination. For all of these are needed if we are going to find ourselves in the right frame of mind, at the right place, at the right time, and then be able to take advantage of all this. Most of us fumble on the first try, and having fumbled on that lose out on the others as well. Yet the rewards even in trying are also great.

If we begin experimenting with being there, it may well be that we will discover how ready the young are to be there to us, too. In fact, it may be they will be the ones to initiate "presence" and help us beyond where we are.

A sixty-three-year-old woman was caring for her father in her home, knowing all the time that he was dying. She had been brought up not to discuss such things, so was unable to say to him all the many things on her mind. She was surprised and deeply relieved to have her college-age son, who was thousands of miles away, call and say he was coming back for a brief time. The son was usually quiet and inarticulate about family matters but this time he went directly to his grandfather's bed and also directly to the point. Taking the frail hand in his, he said very simply, "You're going to go soon, Grandpa, but think of all you have meant. Not many could move into a new neighborhood the way you have and made all those friends. I'm going to miss you, Grandpa. I won't be seeing you again, probably, but I want you to know that I will miss you."

He left. But he had been there in his own way and had not only touched his grandfather but his mother as well. For the first time in her life she felt free to move into her son's frank, free, and open way of saying what was on his mind. After he left and without words, the mother facing her father, was also able to say, *and was heard*—"I, too, know you are dying, and there is much in my heart I want to say to you before it is too late."

It helps, of course, if we can find situations in which we really are of some use. Maybe a foreign student needs to practice his English; or a high school student needs tutoring in a subject we still know well. Perhaps we can get involved in an organization which has some young people in it. The Peace Corps recently sent out a picture of a twenty-eight-year-old man and a sixty-four-year-old woman working together. Maybe we can't do anything which requires as much commitment as that. One of our most important contributions may be no more than not letting other older people, who may be friends of ours, generalize about all young people today as long as we know some who do not fit that generalization.

We have come to the end of our discussion about ways in which our present relationships with kith and kin, friends and strangers offer us fresh opportunities. Much of what is needed from us would seem to depend more on our *being* than on our *doing*. And being, we know, is more subtle, more difficult than doing.

Can we, for example, if we are married, live by the kind of creative love which encourages the other to be a free and becoming kind of person? Can we challenge in our own selves any stereotypes we may have about sexuality in old age? Can we be grateful for the strength of family ties without abusing them? Can we face the reality of social change in family life without taking the consequences of such change personally, blaming and feeling guilty, when understanding of what is happening in society and rational discussion is more what is called for? Can we relate in an adult fashion to our adult children? Can we cultivate an understanding frame of mind towards those in our own generation who are trying out new patterns of life different from our own? Can we find some good friends among the young to discover, past the issue of authority and differing values and life-style, the common humanity which we share?

Can we? Probably we cannot. *Most* probably we cannot. These are huge orders. But there is an exhilaration about contemplating ourselves alongside of huge orders as though, maybe, we were still made for the tackling of some of them. That does not mean we have to succeed. It does mean that they are there, each and every day to be tried. And, even if we fail, the chance to try again will not go away. Relating is an inexhaustible assignment, so great is the need for it in others, so many the persons ready to experiment with us over our own change and growth, so deeply felt the longing for others in our own hearts.

OUR PAST CAN TEACH US

CHAPTER 5

The Life-Cycle Vantage Point

We have been claiming that the past, present, and future of those of us who are older are all basically *for* us. The present tense, we have seen in the last two chapters, offers us some fresh opportunities and resources. In these next two chapters, we will be looking at how our past can benefit us.

Specifically, knowledge of our past can teach us in three ways.

Going back over the several stages through which we have passed in our life cycle can give us perspective on where we are now. How severe are our present problems by comparison? Maybe all trouble is not in the present and all fair weather was not in the "good old days." In fact, are there not moments in old age when we wonder to ourselves, "Haven't we been this way before?" Parallels and precedents in our past can help us guard against self-pity, that special temptation of the closing years.

In doing this we will also be refreshing our memory

on the skills with which we met earlier crises and transition periods. If we coped, we can draw on that confidence and adapt an old skill. If we failed, perhaps we can benefit now from hindsight. Besides gaining a perspective and recalling skills, doing so cannot help but contribute to a "pulling together within us" so that we may begin to feel a strong sense of the "I" who has been there throughout the years.

This chapter will deal with the insights to be gained from comparing our present stage of oldness with two other stages in our life-span. The next chapter will be dealing with this sense of who was there throughout which may emerge when one takes seriously the idea of a personal life review.

Adolescence—Can We Remember?

In old age we feel we are the special victims of stereotyping. We wince over words which have come into popular vocabulary to cover us—senior citizens, oldsters, golden agesters. We feel that we are being lumped together and that the individual who emerges is so homogenized as to be like no one, or that the image reflects only the lowest common denominator.

Have we forgotten? Adolescence is also a word coined to fit a phenomenon and describe an average. None of us wants to be a phenomenon or to feel like an average. Not now. We didn't then. But there was that box into which we were put and the responses it automatically produced—"All teen-agers are . . ." and "She's a teen-ager, that explains it. What else can you expect?" Being stereotyped because of age is not new and in each case we have to resist people attributing to us certain characteristics and making generalizations about us which may or may not be valid.

We say too, that old age has made us unsure about our relationship to society and about how we fit into the mainstream. Was this not true for us when we were in our teens as well? Both old and young have long had a history of being peripheral to the world of those in charge who run things. Both receive funds from sources uninfluenced by what they are doing at the time they are being subsidized. Both have the same relationship to time in the sense that it is relatively unstructured. The pre-employed teen-ager uses time to build up credits for himself against the future. This is a form of marking time. The old are post-employed and are generally seen as wasting time. Again, the young and the old are concerned with their identity and see the family as central to it, but what they expect and want from family is different—the adolescent wanting out of it; the older person, fearing loneliness above all else, wanting to keep in touch with it.

This sense of unsureness about how one fits into things does not intrude itself so much into the other age periods. There is little disagreement over what is expected of a middle-aged adult and what is expected of a child. It is more youth and age who break new ground and are not sure of the boundaries, and it is this which has produced, in both age groups, the same kind of haunting questions. The older person, moving into a category where there are no helpful models or precedents, and where he is given considerable freedom of time, often wonders: What now? What next? Do I belong anywhere? And, more profoundly, therefore, what's it all about anyway?

These same questions stir adolescents. Do we not remember the giddiness and the butterflies in the stomach as a strong feeling of discontinuity with all that had gone before set in upon us? When we left childhood and entered the teens, it was a world which had, overnight, expanded and changed beyond many of the ways we had learned to conceive of it. There were powerful new forces at work which were not only felt to be out there beyond us but also inside us as well. It even felt, at times, as though these forces might have the power to destroy us, and we wondered what they were. We had not been aware of them before. Where did they come from? Were we up to them? And it was all this which brought on that sense of dizzying unpreparedness and awkwardness.

There was also the question of whether we might not have to go back and fight some of our earlier battles over again right when we thought them finished. We vacillated between wanting adult freedom and, when it came into sight and focus, wanting to back away and be a child again, often for much longer than "just for tonight." Yet we were upset that this was so. It was tough having to admit the both-and-ness of our nature even to ourselves.

Is not this much the same kind of upset going on in us now? The clear-cut roles of family and jobs which have held us in place are no longer ours. There is nothing out there to answer the question—What do we do next? What are we here for? What's the point, anyway? Yet this deeply embarrasses, not to say, throws us. We are supposed to be mature, and mature people do not have fears and dreads, or at least they feel they should have some ready-at-hand, experienced way of working them out.

The adolescent, according to Erik Erikson, is one who is not deep-down sure that he is ever going to grow together again. With all the basic decisions still ahead he is not sure he is going to make the right choices without once and for all committing himself to the wrong friend, date, mate, leader, or career. True, this is not quite our fear now, because decisions as basic as those are behind us. But we know well the sensation of things falling apart, the uncertainty of our own place in the busy scheme of things and the deep-down pause as we wonder about motivation adequate enough to carry us through the unknown which lies ahead.

In another sense the two age groups are comparable. As we grow old, one of the unknowns is our body. That was true of adolescence as well. Both periods are a time when physiology predominates. In adolescence, it was not only the rapid change in normal body growth but the onset of sexual maturity that brought on the crisis we faced. We remember how we tried to become attractive and, at the same time, had to learn how to accept our own givens and do the best we could with them—height, weight, features, sex. Our bodies produced new desires and drives in us that frightened, excited, and stimulated, and we were puzzled and intrigued. And then there was our curiosity. We were almost more inquisitive than concerned about the changes taking place. How did our own experience stack up in relation to that of others? Girls clustered in gab sessions comparing notes; boys went off to their rendezvous to tell their jokes.

Now our bodies are older. Once again they are producing in us reactions that frighten and stir up concern and curiosity. We are more tired than we had expected; our energy does not last as long. We must admit to the givens too, and work as best we can around them: changed appearance, bones which do not heal as fast, stiffer muscles and joints, a shrinking body, and wrinkles. We cluster together too, in small groups or pairs, to talk about it and to compare this time, our illnesses and aches.

Moreover, in both cases we are faced with the need to say what we want this new-about-us to be. We had to when we were young. We had to learn to coordinate the rapidly growing set of limbs and make them a part of us so that we could feel, or pose, some poise. We had to learn appropriate outlets for the sexual drive. We had to learn to control the physical processes going on inside us lest they control us.

We must do the same thing now. We must learn to adapt reduced energy to the fact of an aging body, or to a disability, so that again we may have some sense of coordination and poise. We must make our bodies an integral part of ourselves or else "I" will simply become a set of responses to physical cues. What was true for us as adolescents, when we faced integrating our sex drive into our personality, is again true for us now as we try to integrate our aches and pains. Either we will be the kind of person who constantly complains, and the body will run us, or we will be in charge of the body.

Our Middle Age—Parallels and Precedents

Coming closer to home and more recently, our middle age—how does it compare with where we are now?

In old age we know well the feeling of being trapped by the convergence of events, all seemingly against us —widowhood, for example, at a time when we are also losing many of our friends; reduced income when we face the expenses of chronic illness. We complain of feeling helpless. We also feel obsolete. Was middle age devoid of this set of feelings? Were there not times when we looked up from the daily grind, wondered about greener pastures elsewhere in a kind of last call, now-or-never mood but were unable to move? We were bored with *here*, intrigued with *there*, yet decisions made by us earlier and before we had quite known what was happening seemed to have the cumulative effect of locking us into place. We had married, had children, received training, invested in property, taken out policies, signed up for payments. After all that, of course seniority made sense. Made also for a feeling of being trapped.

And in middle age, if one lost his job and looked for new employment, the possibility of obsolescence was not out of the question. True, there was a difference. Being obsolete then did not involve the question we face now of whether we can unlearn something familiar, learn something new, and start afresh. In middle age, the question was more one of whether you could afford the time and money to drop out and begin all over. Nevertheless, though the reasons for obsolescence may have differed, the feeling of being trapped was the same. Anthony Lewis, in *The New York Times* of June 14, 1973, wrote that a man in his Harvard twenty-fifth reunion class filled in a questionnaire circulated before the reunion to the effect that he was owner, operator, and slave of an organic farm of four hundred acres in the middle of nowhere—"Too late," he said, "to turn back; too tired to go forward. Anyone want an overripe tomato?"

Middle-aged women often experienced their own version of being caught "in the middle of nowhere." Said one fifty-year-old mother somewhat wistfully to a daughter just admitted to a medical school, "It takes me back. It came time to be married. It wasn't necessarily planned, but we started going together in high school, and, well, your father was just there all the time so we ended up getting married. It isn't that I didn't like your father but marrying him—*that* changed everything. Before that, I'd always thought I was going to work. Maybe be a doctor too. Seems very long ago and far away, that idea now!"

And what about the feeling of a sense of physical decline and loss? As middle-aged parents, we surely knew the deep discomfort of envy of the young. Though we may never have thought of it as such, was it not there just below the surface? Caught in the moods of their own change-of-life period, as well as in a society which advertises sex appeal and youthful beauty, middle-aged mothers watch their daughters develop. Middle-aged fathers, too, watch and react. They may have reached something of a vocational plateau just about the time they see their sons beginning, vocationally speaking. Reared to win in sports and to thrive on success in the rat race, fathers, too, are not without their intimations of gradual descent as their sons beat them in tennis or come home from school with vocabulary and new information they themselves have not had the time to master.

Of course we wanted our children to surpass us—in education, academic achievement, vocation, physical appearance. That was why we saved and sacrificed. But was there not, also, something of the left-behind feeling hovering around somewhere in the background, when this actually happened? Just as we feel left behind now?

Declining flexibility and becoming rigid is supposed to be particularly true of old people. Is this true? Wasn't the first time it became critical enough for us to notice it sometime during middle age? Was it not then, rather than now in old age, that we first began to detect that faint hardening of the mental and emotional arteries? True, the daily pace of middle age did not allow us to become too set in our ways. We had to appear flexible and up-to-date or we knew we would lose out. But when our children pressed us too hard on the whys and wherefores, or when our job called out for a new touch (not to say a new vision of it), were there not times when we were too tired or tense to make the mental and emotional effort to think up new answers?

And wasn't it in middle age, rather than in our sixties

and seventies, when we began to feel somewhat differently about time—that it was not limitless? We knew loss too. Not in terms of less energy and reduced income as now. But our children left home. We faced loss even before they left when we knew that we were no longer the all-important people in their lives we had been. Often in middle age our parents died and the circle of friends in whom we had invested so much was broken as one or the other moved away, up or down the ladder of success. We knew too, the vertigo that comes when one loss creates a ripple altering things all along the line —children go, so marriage is different, so friends change, so health is affected, so productivity on the job is threatened.

The Life Cycle—Circle or Spiral?

In going back over our adolescence and middle age to compare them with where we are now, we have talked so much about likenesses and similarities we may overlook the fact that old age *is* different. It is the supreme time when negatives converge on us all at once. No other period knows the dread of senility and decrepitude hovering in the background; nor faces death with the same certainty. Moreover, there is a special task unique to each period of life, and ours is described without frills or conditional clauses by Drs. Busse and Pfeiffer, psychiatrists at the Duke University Center for the Study of Aging and Human Development. Their directness is quieting. "The aged person must come face to face with the fact that he is now no longer young, no longer even middle aged but that, instead, he has entered the last phase of his life, the phase which precedes death." So there is, in spite of all parallels and precedents, a special quality to our old age, and mental health requires that we face it.

Unique, but not *that* unique, perhaps. There would seem to be no special dispensation for self-pity which would make that emotion more appropriate for old age than for any other period of life. All stages, as we have seen, have had their frustrations and peaks, their depths, joys, and perplexities. And though there is, especially in this time of rapid change, a strong sense of discontinuity in old age with much that has gone before, have we not already experienced this? Is not *this* very thing the continuity—namely, the deep dismay that is stirred up in us each time we experience lack of continuity between one part of our lives and another? We are not new to this dismay and thus the coping we have brought to it is the continuity on which we can now draw.

Looking back, then, the unique and the special things about old age tend to be balanced by the familiar, or at least by the feeling that it is not a totally foreign experience. It feels as though it belongs in the same way that every other period in our life-span has belonged.

The comparative exercise not only helps us place old age; one comes away from it with a sense of movement, a feeling of how strong are rhythm and alternation, how precious is balance. Balance because there seems to have been so much overlap. In the family, as parents, we were pushed into each new stage as the first child reached it and even while we were still involved with our children in the other stages. Overlap in ourselves too, because one part of us was out there taking us into the growing edges of new experience while another part of us was still trying to finish up with the last stage.

And a sense of rhythm and alternation because one sees how common and how normal are crises. They come. They also go. Evidently all crises are not neurotic, in the sense that all they are good for is to make us waste energy defensively and become more isolated. As we look back and compare, we have seen how some crises, though they may have aroused dormant anxiety in us, have also called forth, and then supported, expanding, growing parts of ourselves. We remember too those times, not quite crises but still stressful, when we were sure we could not move unless the next step was clear. The situation did not clarify. We moved anyway. And we see now, from the vantage point of distance, that something in that very act of moving paved the way for clarification—often not the way we would have prescribed it but a form of clarification nonetheless.

We feel rhythm and alternation, also, because along with crises there were resting periods too. Just before adolescence there was one; again, sometime between twenty-five and forty; and also just before we began to feel old. Buber calls these resting places, in the spiritual life, plateaus; Freud, in his scheme of development, used the words latency-period. In any case, we have known places along the way when there was a chance for us to get caught up.

There seems, too, to have been a little dying throughout. Grief and mourning, evidently, are not confined to old age. Why do we not remember this? Each of us has had to come to terms with so many farewells—to images of self no longer valid; to images of others discredited. We have known the sadness that sexual and physical change in our middle years brings. We were not as brilliant as we had hoped, not as adequate sexually as we had dreamed, not as loving, compassionate, and sensitive as we had prayed. Letting go is something that goes on throughout life, not just in old age. And the letting go of dreams, illusions, and hopes is an experience with a kind of death.

Now in old age we look back at what may have been the greatest example of letting go in our lives—the adolescent letting go of his childhood and taking the risk to leave home; the parent who must participate in letting his or her child go. In any way that we were a party to that struggle, either as teen-ager or again, as parent, we had some prescience of what death must be like and what rebirth may be like.

We began the experience with our children with much touch and cuddliness. We remember how the break began gradually, way back there, when rituals expressing affection, such as kissing the child goodnight, were challenged. "I'm too old for that now, Mom." Then adolescents thought any show of affection was sentimentality and, as parents, we did not dare to show it for fear of embarrassing them. They also cut down on confiding in us and we in turn felt cut off.

But we go back to the beginning. Where did that original sense of intimacy and cuddliness go? It did not necessarily disappear. It changed in form and content.

It changed in us. To be sure, we may have clutched at our children, almost unconsciously, when we realized they were leaving for good, but in time we got our balance again. And so with the family itself. It did not fall apart. Instead, a different kind of family was being born. Perhaps the symbolism of that familiar struggle should capture our attention now, because there was symbolic death in it, while the reconstituting of the family, in whatever way that may have occurred, can be seen as symbolic rebirth.

For us this process has happened three times. We are now old, but many of us were once middle-aged parents of teen-agers presiding over their departure from the family. We are now old, but all of us were once, also, the teen-ager who left the family. We remember, as teen-agers, that our parents really did care in their own way, even though we may not always have seen it in that light; and we remember, as parents, that our teen-aged children cared too. We realize, looking back, that an affection and loyalty of a very enduring kind (and far more than we probably deserved) continued in spite of setbacks and expressions of hostility and angry feelings. What old age makes possible is the highlighting of an underlying caring throughout uneven growth. We see now that even feeling or expressing hostility was a way of saying it mattered. Otherwise no one would have bothered.

We have said that this family struggle was the greatest example of letting go in our lives, but maybe that still lies ahead of us. Maybe those times when we learned to let go in the family with whatever trust and dignity we could muster, were not for that moment only. Maybe they were training grounds for the real letting go which we have yet to face.

There is one question we are bound to ask, after having looked back. Are we a "better" person or a more "grown-up" and more "mature" person now that we have come so far and had the chance to learn so much? There are any number of definitions of successful development, but most of us are not ready to step up and fit ourselves into them. This is not so much due to a sense of modesty, false or otherwise, as to a stronger sense of reality, having gone back over our life cycle. We realize that nothing has been perfected in us. No goodness has been achieved that is fully impervious to conflict; no badness in us that is hopeless. Yet this does not feel like irony, or a joke, or a punishment such as the one meted out to Sisyphus long ago, where we are denied a sense of accomplishment along the way. It feels more like there is an ongoingness about everything.

Though in our poorer moments we may have been tempted to think of the life cycle as a treadmill, even, at times, a going two steps backward for every step forward, we know that, looking back on the whole picture, the circle was not a vicious one. Coming full circle may be an accurate phrase, but it stimulates the imagination as well. Circles need not be endless repetition. They can also be spirals whereby we may reach the same point each time around with the same kind of problems and possibilities present but also at a potentially higher level of human development than before.

This sense of movement tends to make one more

mellow and less judgmental. The ideas of growth and development literally mean that tomorrow he, or she, or I will be different. So we feel less ready to come down hard on someone at any one point in time. We remember that there are plenty of late-bloomers and then, of course, there is our own fragile record.

We are grateful whenever others, against the poor evidence of what were our today-behaviors, yet gave us the benefit of the tomorrows. We remember well those times of testing when we did not do well because we were tired, or sick, or worried, yet there would have been a very different response from us had it been another day. Or worse, when we did falsely because the perverse or the frightened in us got to the surface first and then, once set in motion, it had its own momentum dominating all the sad chain of events that followed. Yet we know that what dominated was not all there was to us and that it might have been different.

Less judgmental and more mellow? This does not feel so much like we are becoming lazy, or are ready to appease, or to give in on values to which we still hold steadfast. Rather, it feels more as though one might slowly be coming into line with the biblical injunction, "Judgment is mine, saith the Lord." We begin to understand that everything really does not depend on us.

Lastly, one feels a sense of rejoicing after having compared the various parts of life. If this is a delayed reaction, and it probably is, it is nonetheless valid. Why so slow in coming to it? Why deep rejoicing now? Besides, there have been some obvious satisfactions all along the way—in our romance, marriage, children, our children's successes, community interests, friends, religious and philosophical explorations, our accomplishments, such as they have been. But this sense of rejoicing is different. It is more total and special and probably for a number of reasons.

For one thing, we need the long view in order to be able to balance things. Quarreling, for example, has a way of going on and on. To express approval, or feel forgiveness, or give a kiss that is genuine takes only moments. We cannot elaborate much on such moments without their cloying. It would seem, then, that even if there have been an equal number of positives and negatives at any one point, the effect has been to make us believe there have been more negatives. It is only as we take the long look back that positives stand out as strong and as distinct, even if more fleeting.

It seems too, that sometimes we can only see and enjoy certain periods when they are all over. Young marrieds can look mighty dull to the young, carefree bachelor. There is no way to tell him, at his point in time, that marriage would not necessarily feel that way to him when he got there. When a person is forty, he or she may fear that, with age, he will become a less desirable sex partner not realizing that, in another decade, the motivation for a highly active sex life will not be as great. Indeed, to tell him that, when he is forty, would only be to increase his apprehension as he looks ahead. There is no way to reach him with the news that, at fifty or sixty, the context is not only different but that the way he will feel about that context is as genuine and authentic for that age as the way he feels now.

And it would seem to be only as we move into the last phase of life that the little and the insignificant, the daily and even the monotonous begin to receive their full due. Up to now, we have tended to compare the ordinary in our lives to the high points and the low and, as long as we have had plenty of time, the ordinary has been just that. But now, in the setting of limited time, we begin to see and to feel all this ordinary in our lives in a quite different way—not as dull, daily routine versus exciting climaxes but as versus no daily routine at all, no more ordinaries ever, in short, as life, whatever its quality, versus life totally gone.

We have been privy to this knowledge all along, of course, so it is not exactly a new threat. But to experience a sense of limited time is quite different from knowing about it. It produces an edge and a special quality to everything we do and feel. We walk out in the morning to the front walk to sweep away the leaves or the snow, but we also stop and take time to realize what we are doing and where we are. We open the window at night to the shadows, movement, and noise of night traffic in the world beyond the window, but we also pause long enough to sense that we ourselves are a part of that scene. Because we are learning to experience the ordinary for what it is—part of a gift which has an end as well as a beginning—new emotions emerge: joy that we have been included to receive the gift, reverence before the mystery that this is so.

We have seen the general themes that have played throughout our youth, our middle years, and now in our growing old. But our lives are not a collection of general themes. They are individual variations on those themes. In the next chapter, we will be exploring more fully one of the ways we can find the unique "I" who has composed, and then played out, his or her own special variations.

CHAPTER 6

Wholeness and the Personal Life Review

It is one thing, at the end of a day, to be asked, "How was it?" and to answer, "Oh, so and so, and this and that." Or to be asked, at the end of a longer period (say a summer vacation, or a couple of years on a job), "Did you have a good experience there? And if so, in what way?" and to answer, "Well, yes pretty good because I felt a bit of this, but a bit of that, too. And this occurred and that was said."

But at the end of a whole lifetime, it will not do to answer, so and so, and this and that, and pretty good. It won't do because it is not all the little have-done's and didn't-do's, and pieces and bits that matter. What matters is *who* was there throughout all this changing panorama of detail—some of it pretty impressive, most of it trivia. *Who* saw fit to perform all this?

112

The Need to Find Who Was There Throughout

There is great need, as one comes to the closing part of life, to find the shape, not of the things we did so much as of the self who did them in the midst of such rapid change and discontinuity. The need, in this instance, is not even to find the worth or the value of the changing self, important as that is, but just the shape. How to bring together the child we were at the beginning of the century, with the present person we now are, and all the changing selves in between? In short, we have our own personal generation gaps to span. And for some there may be the need, as well, to find and bring back into the family of "me" those disowned and rejected parts of self we may not have wanted to acknowledge or remember.

The life-review process is one way for us to put our stamp on the many disparate and dated parts of a puzzle as we say to ourselves, "This little piece, and this, and this, make sense because *I* was there and *I* make sense." It is an essential process for us, in a way, because who else is there to do it? We cannot expect people at our funeral to supply the missing link, nor our children cleaning out drawers, closets, and the safe deposit box after we are gone. They cannot pull together, frame, and feel this person who never was before, and never will be repeated—this "I" who was given a moment in history to do with as he or she saw fit. We cannot expect anyone else at all to find and to know who we are. If it is to be done, it is something that is absolutely and totally up to us alone or else it will not be done—ever.

The Life-Review Process—What, How, and Why

Is the life review a putting together of stray and fleeting bits of the past which pop up in us every so often spontaneously and unbidden—a collection of, "Oh, I just remembered . . ." or "The other night I dreamt of . . ."? Some of this kind of remembering may be intriguing, even significant; most of it is irrelevant to monotonous. In any case, the results are random and without form.

Or is the life-review process a more deliberate type of reminiscence, accompanied by editing, so that the result can be something tangible and of more permanent value? This happens too—all the way from published memoirs of enough interest and written well enough to deserve a wide audience, to the more homey type of bequest— maybe a tape recording of Grandpa's best limericks or a collection of the family's top recipes. This is the fun and satisfying kind of remembering, because everyone gains from it. We hand it over. Someone takes it from us. In the process, both giver and receiver enhance their sense of continuity. It is limited, however, in what it includes and is designed mostly for others to read and to remember us by.

On the other hand, what we have to give *to ourselves* to remember us by is the task of the life-review process. If it is to be effective in helping us to a sense of wholeness it must be more than a commentary on unbidden memories and/or an editing of past events, and it will require from us a persistence and patience, as well as a sense of humor and a nonjudgmental quality about ourselves, which may be a new experience for many of us.

Scholars say that the life-review process is universal among older people brought on by our nearness to the termination of life; by the fact that our defenses are more apt to be down; and by the circumstance that we now have more time than before for reflection. Though there is not too much yet in the way of systematic research on it, interest is increasing.

It is evidently normal in old age to reminisce. Some scholars' findings indicate that reminiscence has no direct relationship either to intelligence or to intellectual deterioration, and that it is *positively* related to freedom from depression and freedom from concern about personal survival. Dr. Robert Butler, who has done a good deal of research on the life review, says that it is prompted by unresolved experiences which people want to relate to and which they want to integrate into their lives. He also says that, if it is taken seriously, a substantial reorganization can occur and that, while there may be a chance for more disorder as we delve into our past, there is also the chance for greater clarity, serenity, and wisdom.

How would one go about the life-review process if one wanted to attempt it? The first step, undoubtedly, would be to expose ourselves to the wide span and variety of the years—*our* years, as we recall all that has gone into them. It could be something like taking a tour over our own property, we being both guide and tourist, and the property being our total life experience. Though the self would be in charge of such a tour, it would not be an ego trip. We are not taking the tour to establish the market value of our property, or to compare our property with other real estate, or even to gloat over some of the best views.

We take the tour because, essentially, we are trying to see our property all at once and as a whole—to understand it, if we can, almost in an ecological sense. We hope to find the delicate balance that exists between all parts of our property—how much old growth is still there and how much new? Where is the running water, where the swampy ground with poor drainage? How much shade is there and how much sun everyday? Where does the land dip and where rise? And the quality of the soil, is it fertile? Will new things grow in it? Do some parts need to lie fallow? Even, we ought to learn (if we can press the metaphor a bit further) what is underground.

How do we set in motion such a tour? There are many things which can prompt us in that direction. Maybe a return to a reunion or celebrating an anniversary. Maybe we go to the attic and there is a box of old clothes, or letters, or cancelled checks. Sometimes the strains from an old, wobbly record like "The Sweetheart of Sigma Chi" take us back, or other sounds as natural and commonplace as rain rattling against a window or trees bending in the wind. Even mirrors. We pass by one and look at ourselves rather casually. We stop. Casually turns to candidly and carefully, and look turns to scrutiny. The contrast between our face now and as we have known it over the years arrests us. It may also start a whole train of thought.

Sometimes it is others who, by their comment or invitation, move us into the life-review mood. On her sixtieth birthday, one of her children wrote their mother a birthday card which read, "We were moved by your comment last Christmas that you have now lived longer than any of the others in your immediate family, and we were moved by your willingness to share that feeling and idea with us. We also feel an excitement, as you set out to chart new paths in the adventure of the sixties. We will be enriched, as in the past, by such sharing of what it means to be you as you can, and want, to share with us. Happy Birthday."

We have been talking about getting a sense of the wide span and variety of our years. But comes a time when we will want to be more selective if we are going to find the one who holds all of it together. Can we, for instance, find some of those experiences (especially early ones) which were strong times, and weak, as far as a sense of self was concerned? When were the times we stood up to a person and took the consequences? When were the times we did not? Can we remember moments when we felt separate, distinct, and absolutely alone and did not run away from that feeling? What about our lies and half-lies over the years, simply because we could not face telling "them" what really happened?

And our fears, how did we handle them? What were we afraid of? The dark, for instance? Can we move into the old paralysis and the terror of that fear again and remember how it ruled us? Did we ever walk into the dark (or whatever was our fear) touching it all over, going right up to it and challenging it, daring it to frighten us any longer? Or, was it a teacher of whom we were afraid? Did she, for instance, make us paint

117

irises and tulips just the way she did, keeping us in line with threats? Did we ever dare resist her in order to paint an iris the way *we* saw it, refusing to change it, taking the bad grade, and accepting the abuse—but still feeling good inside because that iris was *ours*, not hers?

Of course there were the many, many times when we did not make it. We just lay in bed, or sulked in our little corner, and planned strategy which never came off because we did not have the nerve. We need to remember that that individual who did not have the nerve was "I" as much as the brave one. Only as we put the two side by side will we remember the cost involved in process—that it didn't all just happen, like something coming off an assembly line, or following a script in a child development text, but that there was actually a someone, and that someone was "I," who was working away, albeit fitfully, at trying *to be.*

So far we have been talking about remembering what is obvious, acknowledged, and not too painful. Opening up the floodgates of memory, however, can mean for many of us that some things which long ago we put aside as unwanted may now emerge. We do not want them any more now than in the past, but they crop up and will not go away. What to do with them?

One of the wonderful things about growing old, and thus having so much to look back on, is discovering how varied and contradictory are the experiences we have been able to contain. When young, we used to think in terms of blacks and whites. In a sense, it was actually that type of thinking which provided much of our motivation. We didn't like the way our parents and grand-parents ran the country, earned their living, or raised their families. We could do it much better. So we ruled out "their way" and launched forth bravely to debate—sometimes even to try—our way. It was a world of either–or with little tolerance for both–and.

Now, with age, we discover that the opposites are still alive in us, yet we are not torn asunder. Like Walt Whitman who said, "I am large, I can contain multitudes," we can say the same of ourselves. We know perfectly well that the old familiar tugs of war still go on somewhere inside and just below the surface as between the wanting-to-belong-to-others part of us and that wanting-to-be-on-our-own part; as between the breathless, excited, "Oh yes!" part and the tired, fed up, couldn't-care-less part. Idealism and cynicism, compassion and violence are all on tap, yet their coexistence, and our knowledge of their presence, has not destroyed us.

If we can remember this, then we may be ready to face the fact that there may be yet more unfinished business in us to be looked at. Can we approach it in faith, charity, and honesty? Which is to say can we give to our own total self, with *all* its various parts, no less than what God himself gives—understanding, compassion, and forgiveness?

What kind of avoided, skirted, postponed, unexplored parts of ourselves are we talking about, and why should we have them?

In the first place, possibilities for incongruity in ourselves, and the need to keep this incongruity from awareness, are legion in a society where there is so much going up and down the success ladder. Social mobility enforces a kind of transience to the values people cherish and the images they hold of themselves, and this can have poignant overtones of guilt and confusion for the mobile individual in relation to the past which he has left behind.

A short story appeared in one of the large magazines sometime ago, about a fifty-year-old executive who, while facing a crisis in his business, found that the crisis threw him back on the still unresolved question inside of him as to where he felt most "at home." Was it in the house where he was reared, where he still met his mother's gnarled, rough hands and devoted spirit, her poor English, her bedroom slippers on all day, a ketchup bottle on the table, and her readiness to think all he did was wonderful? Or was it in his suburban, ranch-style house, his fashionably gowned wife with manicured hands and vocabulary at ease in the country club and in his business circles, talking about the latest opera and theater? He thought he had successfully exorcised his "limited" background, as well as the child who had grown up in it, but now, in his great need for solace and support, it rose to haunt him.

Sometimes the part of ourselves in the past which we do not want to remember or claim is not so much the result of going up the ladder as going down. This may be due to the contrast between ourselves young, when we were so ambitious, sure, and hopeful, and the way we have actually turned out. We are such a letdown to ourselves now that we would rather not go back and look into that long-ago self who had such high hopes and lofty plans.

Not only the incongruities produced by social mobility but shame, as the result of some painful experience in childhood, may also color an experience in such a way as to make it difficult to find and relive it. Helen Lynd in her illuminating book *On Shame and the Search for Identity* makes an interesting distinction between shame and guilt. Guilt she sees as the result of something specific which we have done. Shame, on the other hand, she feels, is more subtle, more pervasive. It cannot be removed, or made up for by doing certain acts; nor can we communicate it. It comes, she says, not from any big and overwhelming event so much as from an accumulation of the quite trivial. Her examples include being humiliated by an awkward gesture we make; our gauche table manners; the untimely joke that falls flat; ignorance on our part of some unimportant detail which everyone else knows how to handle; the gift which we spent hours on and carefully wrapped to give to an older sibling—only to find it, a few days later, in the wastebasket.

We are ashamed, says Lynd, because of the original episode—yes; but what really eats at us is that we are ashamed to be feeling so deeply about something which should be incidental and slight. That is why shame is difficult to communicate; why, instead, we hug it to ourselves to fester, out of sight.

All of us will undoubtedly have our own experiences of shame—especially those in early childhood—which we will want to take in from out of the cold, warm with a new touch, and with whatever wisdom old age has given us. It is encouraging to have Helen Lynd write that while shame can lead to the belittling of our identity, it is also the kind of experience that, if it can be recovered and fully faced, can then "inform the self."

Review Aftertaste

We have been describing some of the steps in one process which might be followed if we wanted to move from an incomplete and even compartmentalized sense of self to something more total and integrated. What such a strong sense of self leaves us with, however, once it is achieved, varies considerably. Two illustrations will serve to show how different the remainder can be.

In *Krapp's Last Tape*, a shattering, short drama by Samuel Beckett which appeared off Broadway in 1960, old Krapp certainly knew more about himself after replaying the old tape. But the way he felt about that self, after he had looked back over his sixty-nine years, gave him nothing but a sense of waste, as though he had never lived. He felt despair and no fire in him left to combat it, and a "Thank-God-it's-all-done" attitude. On the other hand, Alan Paton, the famous novelist of South Africa, came away from his life review, *For You Departed: A Memoir*, with as strong a sense of total self as had Krapp, but he felt differently about the worth of its past and the potential of its future.

We are introduced to Krapp, and come to know him, through the device of a monologue. Unkempt, unshaven, and forgetful, he sits alone on the stage alongside a small table which has a tape recorder on it. He picks out one tape labeled "Farewell To Love," on which he had evidently recorded his thirty-ninth birthday, and proceeds to play it back to himself. Periodically he turns off the tape to go backstage where we hear the sound of bottle against glass. Then he returns to go on reviewing. He puts special emphasis on his adventures with women, which never seemed to have kindled even the warmth of human kindness to say nothing of love. Except that one glimpse. He goes back to it. The chance for love might have been there he realizes, but it was only for a single moment, and the glimpse so quickly gone only serves now to enhance despair.

Alan Paton's life review says something different about life and the self in it. It is in the form of a book published shortly after his wife's death. Originally, parts of the document were read publicly in Rhodes University Theatre, though a more intimate, frank, and personal account of man's marriage and career can scarcely be imagined.

The book is what is called a kontakion in form, an early Byzantine liturgical chant composed of stanzas and refrains. In the Russian kontakion which Paton knew well, there is a song, the words of which put the crushing pain of sorrow in sober juxtaposition with an alleluia-like affirmation that life is good and finds its proper culmination in death. The book, a life review, follows this juxtaposition. There is humor, matter-of-factness, deep hurt, anger, irony, the depths of grief. The passages move back and forth in time, with the even-numbered passages covering his present, the odd-numbered passages covering his memories of the past.

Again and again, he returns to the stamina and courage (especially during her illness) of the wife who is now departed. Where did it come from, he asks—that which sustained you? He returned again, in memory, to her faith—"that strange Christianity of yours that took seriously the story of the Cross." And throughout this patterned mixing of present with past, shines forth Paton's own faith which also involved, when necessary, the willingness to suffer for what he believed in.

He closes by noting that once before he had written about his grief as though it were over, only to find that it had returned. But now, he says, after this review, it will not return again. Something within was waking in him as from a long sleep and "some immense gratefulness" was returning. "I am full of thanks for life. I have not told myself to be thankful. I just am so."

And what about ourselves if we should try the life review and find the total self coming into clearer focus? Will we feel, like Krapp, a sense of the futility and wastedness of it all, with a burning to be gone? Or will the predominant mood be that of having rounded out something and summed it up, giving us a sense of finality—some kind of benediction to the effort we have made, much like what one senses in old Simeon's, "Lord, now lettest thou thy servant depart in peace."

There is a third possibility. What if the life-review process, in the very doing of it, were to set in motion a new momentum, as seems to have been the case with Paton, so that the sense of closing in and summing up eludes us? What if it were to create new facets of the

"I" not experienced before, so that only the feel of continually breaking ground and growing is left, with something, thus, always to be reviewed, and with the search for wholeness and integrity continuing right up to the end?

OUR FUTURE STIRS UP NEW VISTAS

CHAPTER 7

Givens: Grief and Death—
Not Given: Meaning

The past, as we have seen, calls much to mind. So does our future.

Is it ominous, what our future calls to mind? Our future stirs up in us amazing and provocative images and symbols. It also stirs up in us deep, deep feelings about these images and symbols. Carl Jung wrote, "The head is a particularly inadequate organ when it comes to thinking up religious symbols. They do not come from the head at all, but from some other place, perhaps the heart. . . . Even today we can see in individuals the spontaneous genesis of genuine and valid religious symbols, springing from the unconscious—like flowers of a strange species, while consciousness stands aside perplexed, not knowing what to make of such creations." ("The Soul and Death" in *The Meaning of Death*, ed. Herman Feifel)

Now that we are in the closing third of life, what do we do with these images and symbols stirred up in us, especially those which come in response to contemplating our future? Do we try to capture and pull them back into us, fitting them into the neat and tidy world of good grammar and reason? Or do we let words, rather, be the means of retaining for us something of that beckoning quality which leads us on and on rather than stops us in our tracks? The way the words, for example, of E. E. Cummings often lead us on:

> . . . beyond
> the future's future;and
> immediate like some
> newly remembered dream—
>
> flaming a coolly bell
> touches most mere until
>
> (eternally)with(now)
> luminous the shadow
> of love himself:who's we
> —nor can you die or i
>
> and every world,before
> silence begins a star

In these next two chapters, we will be taking a long look at some of the vistas stirred up in us by our future, because we believe they can take us somewhere worth going.

Thinking and Talking About Death

After the search for wholeness has gone on in us for some time, and when the shape and feel of the "I" is felt, if it is, more clearly (and whether or not it gives us a sense of rounded-out completeness or of continuing openness) there is still the end. We cannot help but remember what lies just ahead of the self and is felt to be closer now than ever before. It is not just *a* loss, or a *few* losses, or several, or that most poignantly felt of all losses—that of our dearest ones. It is, rather, total loss—loss of the self by itself, and it is total because, when that is gone, what is there left for life though everything else may continue to live?

Though death has always been a possibility throughout life, few of us have ever thought much about it. There is a healthy instinct in us which says: Get on with life; when death comes will be time enough. But what now, for us growing old and so much closer to death? Now, when it is not only, or even primarily, our own death but the death of so many others whom we have known—our friends, our peers, in fact, a whole generation? When we go increasingly to funerals and have faced, or know we soon will be facing, the death of loved ones? How can we help but think about death? About what to say to those who are left? About what happens to people after they die? They were just here. Now they are not. Who is there who does not ask the question of himself or herself, at that moment: Where are they now?

So, *not* to wonder, ponder, think about death in these closing years of life may be even more abnormal than to do so. We may not do it out loud, in so many words, so much as in our tossings at night, but that is where our mind is and we can tell. If we can face this; if we can accept the reality that questions and dread are in us, that this is bound to be so especially at this time in our lives, and that having questions and dread and letting them *be* in us will not necessarily tie us to their active consideration continuously—then perhaps we can get on with life in the way most of us want. Yet we will get on with it in a more honest, total—and even relaxed—kind of way than if we had bypassed or postponed the whole issue.

In fact, there is evidence that, in our particular society, when we do not think or have concern about death and dying, it is not because we are treating it in a healthy way, as a natural and normal phenomenon, but because it is a taboo and a deeply repressed one. It is good that, more and more, we are having books and articles published which tell us how people feel when they are dying; how people who attend the terminally ill in the hospitals feel; how families who visit the family member who is dying talk and feel and act; and how parents who want to teach their children early to have a healthy attitude about death might proceed. It is good, too, that as we are exposed to this kind of material about other people, it begins to involve us and to force us to look long and hard at what we find in ourselves as we respond to the research findings.

Maybe *our own* response to the findings is the most important thing. Research in this field is just beginning and, valuable as it is, one wonders, as one reads it, just how much it can really "get at us" and report where we are. One sees studies, for example, which report that old people do not fear death. Yet another researcher points out that to admit to fearing death is not socially acceptable. Only 10 percent in the group he studied admitted to negative or fearful attitudes, while 44 percent were evasive. When the researcher, then, asks for attitudes about death is he getting what people really feel or what they have been brought up and taught to feel?

Moreover, one asks oneself, how would I go about answering a questionnaire on death: "Are you afraid to die? Check here: Yes? No? Uncertain?" We have so many layers on layers built up in us to protect ourselves. As La Rochefoucauld has said, it is like the sun—we cannot really look at it. But perhaps talking with others about it, and feeling more and more free to do this, will help us to peel off some of the many layers which cover up our vulnerabilities. If there are those among us who do not fear it, or who have worked their way through from having feared it to having come to terms with it, then this may make us more able to plumb our own depths. If there are those who have the courage and the honesty to say to us, through the researcher, how they feel at the moment they lie dying, then we can only stand to gain by listening and trying to identify with them.

We can gain not only from research and articulate people who report back to us. Could we ever share, just among ourselves in a natural and informal way, our puzzlement and fears about death? This need not be in the sense of misery loving company so much as mystery making for a common bond among us. For death is our supreme mystery. One other common mystery haunts us as well. Why must we ask the kind of questions for which there are no sure answers? If the universe is unjust, why are we concerned? Where did we get our idea of justice? Why, if we are here solely by chance, do we find in ourselves images which deny our insignificance and pull us toward intent and value, understanding, and truth?

These two mysteries—why meaning is withheld from us about the crucial moment when life meets death and why, then, we are made to seek and long for an understanding of our identity and destiny—are what make us not-animal (for we know more than they) and not-God (for we know less than he). They make us human. They are, quite aptly, spoken of as our predicament.

Would it not make the human predicament more bearable to share it? To do so could not help but relieve the loneliness and the anxiety of selfhood. But the question is, how does one go about sharing it? It is not a simple thing to talk about the puzzlement of who we are, why we are here, and why, soon, we will not be here. Won't doing so only make us sound self-conscious, even phoney and pompous? And we dread sounding like this even more than we dread the bottled-up loneliness of nonsharing.

Nevertheless, some kind of sharing ought to be possible. There are ways of reaching out to let the other person know we know that we are both beholden to the same mysteries and that to seek truth in humility becomes us since we share the same finiteness. It may be better to do this reaching out towards one another through actions rather than through words. Sometimes humor helps. It was the pastor who had gone with heavy step to the Vermont hills to pray for old Asa, lying on his bed for weeks with fever-bright eyes. But the pastor found that *he* came away lighter in heart and spirit because of the way Asa was taking it. "I don't mind goin', not a mite," Asa said simply, "but I do hate t' go in this dilapidated condition."

To talk naturally and informally about death—our death—whether with a wry smile on our lips or not—will depend on temperament and situation. Inasmuch as we are capable of doing it sincerely with each other, whether verbally or nonverbally, it may help us to catch glimpses of meaning in the midst of so much meaninglessness in our lives.

Grief and Participation

We have been talking about sharing our sense of the ultimate mystery with others as a way of helping us both accept the fact of its impenetrability and to be more open to our own feelings about it deep within. What about grief? Is it a private matter? Do we alone participate in it, or is there some point at which participation in it can be shared?

Dr. Robert Kastenbaum speaks of the "bereavement overload" of the old. It is an apt phrase. The older we get, the more we lack the time to work through our grief to a new state of health before we are loaded down once again with the news of another acquaintance, friend, or loved one who has died.

The bereavement overload is compounded because it takes place in an atmosphere where people are uncomfortable about grief. Almost everyone in our society is stilted and clumsy to self-conscious when it comes to expressing condolence. It is not that we are not deeply moved. We are. But the most that seems to come out, all too often, is a perfunctory little note saying, "I'm sorry." Or we take refuge in buying a sympathy card which has our message all printed out for us. Feelings may be there in abundance; love, warmth, and sympathy may well up inside of us, but our words, whether written or spoken, are usually sparse or in cliché form.

Moreover, we are embarrassed in the presence of someone who has broken down and is showing his grief emotionally. At a recent conference of professionals meeting for a symposium on "Ministry to the Dying and Bereaved," one of the speakers, a registered nurse, suddenly lost her composure in the midst of a very calm presentation when she mentioned that one of her colleagues had lately died. The audience stared at the floor and was very tense until she regained her composure. Later, the speaker who followed her commented on the incident in view of the topic they were met to discuss. He admitted how he felt. "I felt like, let me out of here. I got very uncomfortable and thought, please get over that. Please stop." He went on to say that, brought up as he was to control his emotions and often to hide them, he could not face anybody else's emotions.

It is good, therefore, especially for those of us who are growing old and are faced with an overload of bereavement, that we are learning more than we have ever known before about the grief process—both its psychological and its spiritual aspects. We are learning that grief takes much longer than either public opinion or official mourning periods have usually allowed for it; that there is no one correct pattern into which to press our various agonized responses; that crying is not effeminate and that breaking down and sobbing is not a sign of weakness or self-pity; that expressing our grief, and the rage and guilt and depression which often go with it, is not only appropriate for all ages and both sexes, but that it may be a necessary stage on the way to recovery for many. We are even learning, according to Elisabeth Kübler-Ross in her book *On Death and Dying*, that the dying person also goes through the grief process and that it is not, as some of us may have thought, confined to those who sit by the bedside mute and helpless. The dying person also faces leave-taking; he is losing loved ones too; he also mourns.

To know the psychological facts about the grief process is one thing, but to go through the process is quite another. Can this be shared? Grief is different. It is a private matter.

Perhaps it would be more accurate to say that it begins as a private matter. This is not to say that we are isolated. Others come into our lives, when grief comes, to help and to comfort us, and we receive, gratefully, out of our need, their love and concern. But this is not a sharing of our grief. By the time we are ready to open up and share, in any real sense of that term, what is as deeply personal as our grief, healing has already set in.

Before healing, though—or even wanting to be healed—no one can spare us. Grief requires our full participation every step of the way, and the despair of grief's depths cannot be shared. The darkness of its valley of the shadow cannot be bypassed or gone around. We must go into the depths by ourselves and find our own way through the valley. We may hear about the grief of others, but what we hear is "out there." We may know, in theory, that grief exists in our neighbor's heart and house, and on the battlefields of the world; we cannot let this knowledge come in to where we are. We are not ready to broaden our horizon. In fact, we need to turn in upon ourselves and hug our grief to us. It is a form of hugging to ourselves, so that he or she will not be lost, the loved one who has died. Don't let the vivid memory fade. Don't let me forget. Don't open me up or distract my attention. Leave me alone. I mourn.

We may sense, at that point in the process and with some instinct for health and survival buried deep in us, that beyond the present pain and numbness an opening up of ourselves is going to have to take place sometime and that only we can accomplish it. We may hear the still, small voice inside warning that, sooner or later, we are going to have to let go and learn that the loved one is gone forever; that death is real; that the break will have to be clean, the farewell complete, and the memory placed and loved—not hugged. But we are not ready for that learning yet, and it is crucial that this learning, when it comes, be authentic. It must come from the inside out and not be "put on," like a mask, because we think "it's about time," or because others think we "should" so we do it "for their sake" and more with their words and concepts than our own. It must be *our* timing and *our* words and concepts, lest the comfort prove premature, the assurance we give ourselves too cheaply bought.

In James Agee's novel *A Death In The Family*, the young mother, as she gets dressed for the funeral of her husband, is amazed at her own poise since his going. She had been taking comfort from the fact that she was enduring, assuring herself that grief happens to many, that she had never before realized how strong human beings could be, or how great was the might and tenderness of God. She felt as though she had grown up overnight. So, of course, when it came time to put on her veil and leave the bedroom for the church she was sure she was ready. It was only as she saw herself in the mirror, as she was about to leave the room—which meant, she suddenly realized, leaving the shape of her existence up to that point forever—that what had really happened came to her. She was not ready at all. Her fine, mature image of herself evaporated into thin air, and all she could do was to double deeply over, "hands to her belly, and her knee joints melted."

The familiar, comforting words and rituals—even God's presence—cannot help if we conceive of them as relieving us of participation or as leading us around, or over, rather than into and through the valley full of shadows.

There comes a time, though, in this journey that goes through rather than around, when we begin to feel that our direction is more *out of* than *into*. One of the ways we can tell whether this is so is when the music of Bach's Mass in B Minor, for example, floods in on us and we no longer hear it as a mass for just our own grief—a me-and-mine kind of music—but as deeply human music which moves us into an understanding of how universal is the particular we are going through.

Or again, we can tell that we are moving up out of the valley when we find ourselves relating to the grief of others, not so much in order to lean on them as out of a growing awareness of our own new balance, strength, and insight, and our readiness to give out of this. It is those who have gone through, rather than around, who are unique in their ministry to the bereaved. A widow, for example, can help a widow in a way no one else can.

It may also be that we will begin to feel our grief not only as an integral part of our human heritage, but as having cosmic overtones as well. We look at the face of the mother in Michelangelo's unfinished Palestrina Pieta, looking down at the rough, rugged, limp body of her dead son sagging on her lap. Michelangelo did not finish her face. We are almost glad he did not. The hints he does give us and the shadows that play across the Madonna's roughly hewn countenance are enough. They draw us out of our hugging mood and we quietly "finish" her face by identifying our own with it.

We look at a picture of the medieval wooden statue done by Riemenschneider, where God the Father sits on his small wooden throne holding his dead son. Even with the stiffness that goes with wood and the formalized pose that goes with that period, here is a face of such anguish, with its slightly quizzical quality, that it pulls us up out of our depths and stretches our horizon. The two greatest biblical symbols—the Suffering Servant and the Cross—teach us that it is not just I, nor even all humankind, but that God himself is a God who is acquainted with grief and knows its sorrows.

Painting Heaven Differently

The mysteries inherent in our human predicament as well as our feelings about death and dying, and our grief —we have seen that each of these offers the possibility of being shared, but in special ways if our sharing is to have a growing edge to it. What about beliefs and doubts regarding life after death? Can they be shared? Or don't people even think about the hereafter anymore? To ponder and to wonder about it has been a real part of what being human has meant.

Animals may or may not grieve. Jane Goodall, in reporting on her life with the chimpanzee in East Africa, says that she has seen a mother chimp holding her dead baby for days, gazing at it without moving or eating. So it may be that animals do mourn. As far as we are aware, though, animals do not know, throughout their life, what lies in store for them. Nor do other animals gather round, when the end is finally consumated. *We* know. We carry the knowledge with us throughout a lifetime and we gather round, when it happens to our fellows, to perform some kind of ritual or ceremony, or to make some kind of mark.

The human animal buries his dead. The human being is the first animal to do so. When some animals began to do this, they had a prescience or "knowledge" that distinguished them from other animals. One could almost say, if one could collapse eons of time into a single moment, that at some indistinguishable point in prehistory, an animal lifted up one foot and put it forward somewhere and from then on there were creatures on the face of this earth who straddled two worlds. That creature was no longer "innocent" as the Bible says. Or, to put it positively, there was a plus about the human animal. He knew.

But his knowing was only in part. He knew that he was bounded by time, that he was mortal, and that he would surely die. He was not told the why or the wherefore of his mortality or whether immortality was in store for him. It is man's partial knowledge that has set his mind to spinning in faith and his ears to listening, beyond the noise of earthquake and fire, for the still small voice.

A young woman visiting in Africa was having a serious bout of malaria. In the middle of one of her delirious periods, she opened her eyes, turned her face towards the friend by her bedside and said, quite lucidly, "When I contemplate infinity I get just so far, and then I can't cope. It boggles the mind. I get dizzy." Having said that, she turned away, and the friend was left to wonder: Wasn't the dizziness from malaria enough? Why this extra dizziness? Why were human beings made to carry such imaginings, such visions, such gropings as they do? Yet they have had them for as long as we have had recorded history. They still have them today.

Studies show that many older people believe in some form of immortality, but some do not. It would be interesting to know what those who believe mean by that and what those who do not believe also mean. And have people's beliefs about eternal life changed? Have new events battered away at cherished concepts? Have those who have not believed in a personal form of immortality but have, for example, believed that we continue on through children, through friendships, through creative contributions to the culture, or through a nation for which one has sacrificed—have they felt any change in their convictions now that we face the possibility of total nuclear annihilation? Likewise, have other new events reaffirmed old beliefs? Has space exploration or the renewed interest in Oriental religions opened and stretched people's thinking about life beyond this life?

Could we share our thinking and beliefs or, if we do not have anything as clear-cut as beliefs, could we share with each other at least where we are now? It is true that pooling our ignorance and our hangups would only confound us; and bringing a set of rigidly held dogmas to be imposed on a group would not help either. But again, as with our feelings about the human predicament, death, and grief, so with whatever it is we believe about what happens after death—there ought to be a way we can reach and help each other and be enriched by the sharing.

Carl Jung has reminded us that one of the oldest facts about human beings and what distinguishes them from other animals is our regarding death "as the fulfillment of life's meaning and as its goal in the truest sense, instead of a mere meaningless cessation." "If," says Jung, "from the needs of his own heart, or in accordance with the ancient lessons of human wisdom, or out of respect for the psychological fact that telepathic perceptions occur, anyone should draw the conclusion that the psyche, in its deepest reaches, participates in a form of existence beyond time and space, and thus partakes of what is inadequately and symbolically described as 'eternity' . . . he would have the inestimable advantage of agreeing with a trend of the human psyche which has existed from time immemorial and is universal in incidence." (from "The Soul and Death")

One of the oldest facts about man, too, as we know him in human history, has been his image-making about life after death: buildings built for burial, like the pyramids of Egypt and the beehive tombs of Mycenae; and pictures of what the environment and the daily routine of life after death would be like—shadowy regions around the river Styx and the Christian heaven and hell.

Do we have no images today? But of course we do. The concepts of total cessation or nothingness are images and, in their way, as specific about what to expect as any painting on an Egyptian tomb with its boats and chairs and cosmetic vases, or as any carving on a medieval cathedral with its gates and angels and trumpets. The idea, so popular today in our secular society, that the hereafter is not important—that it is, even, irrelevant —is saying as much about "what it is like" as the biblical view that it is a state of things where peace and justice prevail.

Image-making has been the special province of the artist. We find enormous variety as to the meaning of death and what the hereafter is like, not only among periods within the history of art (such as the ancient, medieval, and modern periods) but within a period itself.

In modern art, Van Gogh pictures a figure with a scythe, mowing down corn. He says, in one of his letters, that the reaper is the image of death but that there is nothing sad about it. All this takes place in a cornfield, in broad daylight, where the sun floods everything "with a light of pure gold" even as the cornfield disappears into the distance.

Manet, on the other hand, in his painting entitled *Funeral,* presents what is happening as a minor event, something quite anonymous, "lost in the landscape," a procession which is merely another "glimpse caught of man's world on a rainy day." Chagall pictures the greatness of the afterlife in his painting *Mirror* in which his wife, Bella, a tiny figure, is shown having fallen asleep beside a table, while in the background in a mirror overhead is a large reflection of a lamp, symbol of eternal light. These and other insights into images of life and afterlife are discussed by Carla Gottlieb in her essay "Modern Art and Death."

To talk about the variety in man's images of the hereafter, whether in art or in other forms, is not to ridicule the fact of human inconsistency, nor is it to imply that, since there is so much variety, the concept must be nothing more than a product of man's imagination. In the most profound sense, it is to say that man is an image-maker. There is no other way we humans can think or say things about the intangibles and the ultimates, either to each other or to ourselves—most particularly to ourselves—except to do so in images.

Also, we do not know for sure. This is the burden and the challenge of our finiteness, but this burden and this challenge are not always accepted. When one book tells us that it is important for parents and teachers to help the child face reality and realize that death is final and that there is nothing after death, one is tempted to ask: Where does the author get his evidence for such a dogmatic statement? Why not leave the door ajar? Or at least say to the child, "This is my belief. Others believe quite differently. And no one can be certain." Yet we know that, probably only fifty years ago, the statement about what to teach a child would have been just the opposite but in the same dogmatic vein.

It would seem, then, that there are at least two things to remember if we want to make a sharing of our concepts about what happens after death a mutually helpful experience. One would be to recognize that the only way we human beings can grasp or depict reality is through images. But we do not confuse our images with reality itself. We also do not assume that, because we can only think about reality in images, this means reality itself is just an image, or a product of our imagination. Moreover, if we are to gain in such a sharing, we will have to come to it in a seeking spirit. Our presence would be not for the purpose of trying to persuade others about the absolute rightness or accuracy of our particular view of the hereafter. Rather, it would be to learn more about the rich imagery which each individual brings to the abiding mystery and what the faith and resources of each means to him or her as he turns his face in the direction of meeting the final crisis.

It is interesting that, even among those who have had great faith and have been near death, we still find a wide variety of images. The aged John, on the island of Patmos, pictured heaven most vividly in his book of Revelation, with its streets of gold and its fountains of crystal. Dietrich Bonhoeffer, the German pastor writing in his *Letters From Prison* during the Second World War, thought of what lay ahead after his execution as a great feast. C. S. Lewis pictured it as a huge room where rational mind was predominant. For T. S. Eliot, in his *Four Quartets*, it was a darkness that would turn to light, a stillness that would turn to dancing, an end that would be where we started from.

It was not the image each of these individuals held, however vivid, but the assurance they felt of God's continuing love and concern which undergirded their faith. It was their conviction that no height nor depth, neither life nor death, could separate them from this. And it is this which can make the crucial difference for us too. It can slowly change our questions for one thing. Not why so abrupt an end, with no clue. Not what is it going to be like in the hereafter. But whom does one know to believe in, and how can we learn to relate to His presence more wisely here and now?

CHAPTER 8

Human Perspective, Eternity, and the Eternal One

We ended chapter 7 with the words, "how to relate to His presence more wisely." This implies that we have been maintaining a meaningful and vital relationship with God throughout our lives and only need to improve it. For many this is true. For others, it may be both true and not true. And for others it is not true at all.

The Eternal Dimension of Our Lives

How we conceive of the Eternal One and what we think the essence of the human-divine relationship to be constitute what we mean by the eternal dimension of our lives. It also includes how we conceive of time and eternity. We will look at our thoughts and feelings about the Eternal One first.

Some meet life and death with dignity and courage in the face of what they believe is cosmic indifference. They draw on resources within themselves and to be found in others—both in their friends and in the witness of human history. As they share, out of their integrity and the sincerity of their belief, their lives are a blessing to those who know them. Some meet life and death with the steady conviction that God is the divine source of life and love. They believe that God transcends this world and that he has an individualized, never-failing love for all his creatures, such as Christ showed to the lost, the last, and the least. Such persons are, in every sense of that term, a godsend to those who know them. Others have faith in God, but faith does not come easily. They have deep longing and growing certitude, but this is punctuated by question, doubt, and struggle. To paraphrase Augustine's famous phrase, "I am restless until I find my rest in Thee," this kind of person could say to the Eternal One, "I am restless *in* Thee."

There seems to be another group, large and growing, which author John Meagher refers to as "the ungifted." Gifted in love and hope, yes. But ungifted when it comes to the third of that trinity—faith. Theirs is not so much unbelief as "loyal undisbelief" says Meagher in *The Gathering of the Ungifted*. They are not hostile to faith but, because they are honest, they have to say it lacks vitality in their case. They feel, when they pray, that it is more monologue than dialogue. Others, they know as skilled, sensitive, and effective in the matter of faith. They, the "ungifted," feel unskilled, especially in the matter of "hearing" since they do not sense the affirmation, guidance, comfort, and forgiveness they long for and which others seem to receive.

Being ungifted in the matter of faith does not mean a lack of interest in it or a rejection of it. Genevieve Gennari, in her autobiography, *The Other Woman I Am*, says that, although she went to parties and was daily involved in practical and pressing issues, there was always underneath, somewhere inside of her, a debate going on over the most important questions she felt human beings could ask: Is there a God? Does he care? Can I find him? These same questions, as Peter Berger has shown in *The Precarious Vision*, can still be there but asked quite differently: What if it just happened to be true that the universe is *not* a mindless machine destroying all within it? What if death *should* turn out to be *not* the ultimate reality of the human phenomenon?

These are the questions of which we are never free, and the way we decide to answer them (for even a no-answering is a form of answering) forces us to develop an eternal dimension to our lives.

This dimension includes not only our belief about the Eternal One but also our concept of eternity as well. Time and place require a new questioning from us who soon will no longer be in the *here* and the *now* and who are discovering daily that nothing is forever.

What do we mean by eternity? We need to place ourselves in relation to a larger dimension, but what? In a *New Yorker* cartoon recently, there appeared the picture of an elderly couple, well winged, haloed, and sitting on a cloud. The husband, in the middle of reporting on something, had evidently begun to sum up, for the wife was objecting. "But up here, Henry, there's no need to make a long story short." Is this what we mean by eternity—an endless future, very much the same as here?

Lest we fall into absurdities and self-deception, perhaps the most honest and accurate thing for us to do, when we try to describe eternity to ourselves, would be to give our imagination full rein within the given fact of mystery. But just because we cannot define eternity, or describe it adequately, is not to say that it is not a reality. We were made to be aware of it and aware of it we are.

We know that we are aware because we are able to stand off from our "prison" and ask its meaning. We are not without glimpses of what eternity must be like. There are split seconds when, as in Edna St. Vincent Millay's *Renascence*, we are privy to a God's-eye view of things. But it is too heavy a weight to sustain for long. Sometimes there are "signals of transcendence," as Peter Berger says in his book *A Rumor of Angels*. But to detect such signals one must be willing to follow the rumors and to be open to where they may lead. It is not always easy to be open and to follow.

C. S. Lewis gives us the example of his wife who spent a morning being sure God wanted to ask her to do something, but being sure, also, that it would have to do with some "tedious duty or sin." She postponed for as long as she could. When she did give in she was surprised to hear that the Lord wanted to give her something instead, and, says Lewis, "Instantly she entered into joy."

Simone Weil once put two words into intriguing juxtaposition: "gravity and grace." To experience gravity in one's life is to know that one is fully involved in the natural order of things and held to historical time and space by a force we can neither deny or defy. God's graciousness, on the other hand, puts us beyond the limits of the here and now by our participation in a relationship with him who stands before and beyond our lives and our world as the ground of all existence.

Straddling two worlds may not be the most comfortable position but, more than any other, does it not do justice to the facts that make up our human condition? Here and now we are, with feet very much on terra firma, but our equilibrium responds too, to a ground underneath, the ground of all existence, beyond this time and this space. We call this other ground eternity.

The Eternal One and Historical Experience

There is more to the eternal dimension of our lives than just our own personal experience (or lack of it) with the Eternal One and our own personal concept of time. Our lives are set in a context of historical experience, and the Eternal One is a very real part of that experience. While each of us answers his or her questions primarily in the light of personal experience, we need to include the experience of others in our total consideration.

We begin with the fact that, centuries ago, a great "knowledge" was born in human beings that God is One, that he commanded there be no other gods before him, and that from the viewpoint of eternity, human beings mattered. When human beings began to realize that there could be a dialogue with God, rather than a relationship of propitiation, or as the Greeks saw it, helplessness before Fate, their reverence and obedience, love and concern began to supplant fear, appeasement, and the use of magic. Moreover, what makes the biblical record so challenging, whenever we are prone to slip into thinking that God is a projection of the human imagination, is that this historical record of the great I Am, breaking through, jarring, disturbing, commanding, surprising, affirming, forgiving, and throughout, refusing to disappear from the human psyche, is a record which shows God as more than what people, at any one point in history, either were comfortable with or wanted.

God was not only a voice which people did not always want to hear. The image of him which came across often violated what people expected of divinity. God a carrier of burdens? God not in the power-making events such as earthquake, wind, and fire but, rather, in a still small voice? God not in a specific temple of stone or marble because the temple of God was within human beings? The Messiah born in a stable? God himself could suffer? Vulnerable because he loved? God called men to the truth because the truth could set men free? Freedom and truth, when all that the world had known for centuries were dictators and slaves?

Thus, a persistent kind of beyond-human authority shines through the varied experiences of God reported by biblical men and women. They knew a voice which had called them forth to be more than just what their culture had taught them to be and, bound by time and their upbringing, they could only feel that such a voice must have eternal qualities to it. Since it created new things within them they felt its source was the Creator.

What, then, in summing up, shall we say of the eternal dimension in historical experience?

It is composed of tensions, longings, chords, and echoes in us far beyond what society alone sets in motion or what we can think up all by ourselves. The evidence is that throughout history human beings have longed for and sought after God. People have also testified that they have found an answer—that they have heard a voice and felt a presence. It is a voice which calls human beings to transcend themselves, often at great cost, haunting them with the difference between where they are at any one point and where they ought to be. It is a presence which has encouraged with love, healed with forgiveness, and judged with compassion.

Yet always human beings have experienced a special, alive kind of quality in the voice and the presence, for the Eternal One is one who smashes idols and challenges the human propensity for idols. He thrusts us out beyond our limited selves to seek his image all over again, to learn how to pray to his own eternal self, not to the God we imagine, and to grow in that whole process. George Macdonald, born in Scotland in the last century, wrote in *The Diary of An Old Soul* this prayer, beyond time and place in its appropriateness:

> Be with me, Lord. Keep me beyond all prayers:
> For more than all my prayers my need of thee,
> And thou beyond all need, all unknown cares;
> What the heart's dear imagination dares,
> Thou dost transcend in measureless majesty

Human Perspective, Eternity, and the Eternal One

All prayers in one—my God, be unto me
Thy own eternal self, absolutely.

Time for the Eternal at Our Age in This Society

We have going on inside us many processes by which we may reach out to the eternal. There is the thought process, the creative process, the wonder-ponder process, the being-thankful process. We have already spoken of the grief process which, psychologically and spiritually, must now be met by us more and more.

As one grows old, one says to oneself, I have to have time—I have to make more time to work through, if I can, what some of these things mean to me. Why was I made to wonder and weep? For that matter, why was I made for laughter, panic, joy, forgiveness, rage, worship, and lust?

But time we have. That is the one thing we have in abundance. So why speak of having to "make" time to work through some of these things? There must be hesitancies in us. What holds us back? Is it because we are afraid that if we carry on this kind of activity it will only isolate us further from where the action is, fitting us all the more into the pious, folded-hands, rocking-chair image? Or is it because we sense that it will require a deliberate and conscious decision on our part which means in turn, energy and discipline, as well as time, if we are going to stick at it?

In either case, we face the fact that the eternal dimension is not a popular one. For most of us, just the idea of taking time out to think is enough to drive us up a tree, to say nothing of thinking about eternal matters. Popular or not, however, there is some evidence that we do it anyway. But how good we feel about doing it and how creative we are in it is not clear. Perhaps that is because our society is not the kind to see eternal explorations as relevant. A materialistic, secular society does not encourage meditation and prayer, nor does a productive, profit-motivated, activist-oriented society support time out for personal introspection and contemplation.

Why, then, do we think of doing it? We do it—those of us who so choose—because, quite simply, this is where we feel we are. The ultimates are not to be put off. We know all about wanderings of the mind, the pressures on us of what others think, our own propensity for dawdling. We know, too, the urgency of our inner longings. We feel we have a job to do in and on ourselves. We need to center down, to use the vocabulary of the saints; or to "know thyself," as the philosophers put it. As we have seen, we need to bring our past up-to-date and to graft it into our present to make us whole. Above all, we need to find meaning in life's ending in order to give it dignity and to leave a benediction behind us.

Moreover, to explore the ultimates is more than doing a job just on ourselves. Actually, it is conviction about the ultimates and commitment to that conviction, which is an important source of motivation to go beyond ourselves to others. Bernice Neugarten has said that for old people today all their reason for being and motivation must come from within, because society, in effect, does not care. But where do we go to develop and strengthen that "within"? The eternal dimension speaks to it, but always it places our "within" within something bigger—the context of our fellowmen and of God.

For some, this pursuit of the ultimates will be an already familiar experience. They have been faithfully involved in its discipline and excitement all their lives, and they go on with it, in their closing years, to further a seeking well begun, very much in the spirit of Pablo Casals who, when he was asked at age ninety why he practiced eight hours every day answered, "Because I think I'm improving." Others may be moved—spurred even—by a sense of adventure since, due to our societal taboo on nonactivist behavior, all of this may be relatively unexplored territory for them. For most who decide to do it, though, it will probably be because, as was the case for the life review, we have never had before this same combination of leisure time coupled with a sense of vulnerability and readiness.

Just as our starting points will be different, so will there be variety in the ways we go about it. For some, this will be mainly through genuflection, ritual, and worship with a like-minded group; for some through regular moments of silence and withdrawal; for others mostly in rational discussion and thought. And yet others will not proceed in any of these ways but will seek and find in body movement, exercise, and in the celebration of laughter, song, and dance.

We must not forget the potential in such humble dailies as the preparation of food for others and the scouring of pots and pans. There is good classical authority that this can be a rich source of spiritual insight in the seventeenth-century devotional *The Practice of the Presence of God* which consists of conversations with an unlearned man, Brother Lawrence, who spent his life, barefooted, in the kitchen of a monastery and experienced God there.

There are then many paths to the living God, and we are free to choose one way or a combination of ways. But no matter which way we choose, if we plan to take the eternal dimension of our lives seriously, we will be prepared to give time to it. We will also proceed with imagination, even—almost—with a sense of lightness and abandon in our step, as though responding to rhythms being played far off in the distance which are, at the same time, deep down inside of us as well. In this spirit we can respond to God.

We have tried in this book to think positively and realistically about the three tenses of our lives—in this case the closing years of our lives in this particular society. There will come a time when we will close all tenses. We can choose to believe that, when that time comes, we will not be beyond His presence whose dimension is greater by far than our time and space and above our imagining. Describe in words what this "not being beyond His presence" means? Explain the mechanics of it? Support the faith with logic and empirical evidence? Paint convincing symbols of what it will look like? None of these we can do. We can neither say this is the absolute truth, nor can we say, absolutely, that this is not the truth.

Not knowing, we are left free to choose. We are free too, to make the costly discovery that it is only as we live into our chosen faith—in fact, begin to turn over our very self to it—that we can experience the full lift of its grace and the strength of its renewing power.